FabJob®

BECOME A
BOOKSTORE
OWNER

BY GRACE JASMINE

FABJOB® GUIDE TO
BECOME A BOOKSTORE OWNER
by Grace Jasmine

ISBN 1-894638-76-X

Library and Archives Canada Cataloguing in Publication

Jasmine, Grace
FabJob guide to become a bookstore owner / by Grace Jasmine.

Accompanied by CD-ROM.
Includes bibliographical references.
ISBN 1-894638-76-X

1. Booksellers and bookselling—Vocational guidance. I. Title.
II. Title: Bookstore owner.
Z283.J38 2005   381'.45002   C2004-905743-X

Important Disclaimer: Although every effort has been made to ensure this guide is free from errors, this publication is sold with the understanding that the authors, editors, and publisher are not responsible for the results of any action taken on the basis of information in this work, nor for any errors or omissions. The publishers, and the authors and editors, expressly disclaim all and any liability to any person, whether a purchaser of this publication or not, in respect of anything and of the consequences of anything done or omitted to be done by any such person in reliance, whether whole or partial, upon the whole or any part of the contents of this publication. If expert advice is required, services of a competent professional person should be sought.

About the Websites Mentioned in this Guide: Although we aim to provide the information you need within the guide, we have also included a number of websites because readers have told us they appreciate knowing about sources of additional information. (**TIP:** Don't include a period at the end of a web address when you type it into your browser.) Due to the constant development of the Internet, websites can change. Any websites mentioned in this guide are included for the convenience of readers only. We are not responsible for the content of any sites except FabJob.com.

FabJob Inc.
19 Horizon View Court
Calgary, Alberta, Canada T3Z 3M5

FabJob Inc.
4603 NE University Village #224
Seattle, Washington, USA 98105

To order books in bulk phone 403-949-2039
For media inquiries phone 403-949-4980

www.FabJob.com

About the Author

FabJob Guide to Become a Bookstore Owner was written by Grace Jasmine with contributions from Jennifer James and Patricia R. Tegtmeier.

Grace Jasmine, an award winning author and business owner, has spent the last fifteen years working directly with bookstore owners and publishers. As a career counselor, Grace has helped hundreds of clients become clear about their dream jobs and define the steps required to realize their dreams.

For the *FabJob Guide to Become a Bookstore Owner*, Grace Jasmine has picked the brains of "who's who" in the bookselling industry and gleaned the best and most useful insider information for you in this powerful how-to book. This informative guide will take you from your initial idea of opening an independent bookstore, through the first day you open your doors, to the day you realize that you are a success!

Acknowledgements

Naturally, a book like this requires the expert knowledge of many astute and erudite people.

I would like to thank **Oren J. Teicher**, Chief Operating Officer of the American Booksellers Association for his insight and advice. I am also indebted to **Suzanne Brooks**, President of the Canadian Booksellers Association for her advice and acumen.

Additionally, the friendly wisdom and the real-life experience of the many successful independent booksellers and book industry professionals who were gracious enough to talk with me added invaluably to this text. They are:

- **John Brancati**
  Owner, East End Books
  East Hampton, New York

- **Thom Chambliss**
  Executive Director
  Pacific Northwest Booksellers Association

- **Susan Dayus**
  Executive Director
  Canadian Booksellers Association

- **John Glazer**
  Chief Executive Officer
  Praxis Bookstore Group LLC
  Little Professor Book Center

- **Donna Paz Kaufman**
  Owner, Paz & Associates
  The Bookstore Training & Consulting Group

- **Mary Ellen Kavanaugh**
  Former Owner, My Sisters' Words
  Syracuse, New York

- **John King**
  Owner, John K. King Used and Rare Books
  Detroit, Michigan

- **Tim Morell**
  Owner, Take One! Film and Theater Books
  West Hollywood, California

- **Al Navis**
  Owner, Almark & Company Booksellers
  Toronto, Ontario

- **Gayle Shanks**
  Co-Owner, Changing Hands Bookstore
  Tempe, Arizona

- **Mary Gay Shipley**
  Owner, That Bookstore in Blytheville
  Blytheville, Arkansas

Special thanks to contributing author **Patricia R. Tegtmeier**, sole proprietor of A Novel View®, an independent bookstore in Anchorage, Alaska.

Contents

1. **Introduction** 1

   1.1 Welcome to Bookselling 1

      1.1.1 Traits of Bookstore Owners 1

      1.1.2 What Bookstore Owners Do 3

      1.1.3 Benefits of This Career 8

   1.2 Inside This Guide 9

2. **Learning The Business** 11

   2.1 The Language of Bookselling 12

   2.2 The Book Industry 15

      2.2.1 Who's Who in the Book Industry 15

      2.2.2 The Life Cycle of a Book 18

   2.3 The Books 23

      2.3.1 Parts of a Book 23

      2.3.2 Book Categories 25

   2.4 The Bookstores 28

      2.4.1 Where Books Are Sold 28

      2.4.2 Types of Independent Bookstores 30

   2.5 Developing Your Knowledge and Skills 40

      2.5.1 Mystery Shopping 41

      2.5.2 Contacting Bookstore Owners 46

      2.5.3 Working in a Bookstore 49

      2.5.4 Booksellers Associations 49

      2.5.5 Educational Programs 56

3. **Planning for Your Bookstore** 61

   3.1 Identifying Your Ideal Bookstore Type 61

   3.2 Imagining Your Bookstore 65

      3.2.1 Visualizing Your Bookstore 65

      3.2.2 Describing Your Bookstore 66

      3.2.3 Creating a Picture of Your Bookstore 68

   3.3 Setting Your Goal 72

3.4 Moving from a Goal to a Plan 75
    3.4.1 Brainstorming 75
    3.4.2 Using Checklists to Get Organized 75
    3.4.3 Creating an Action Plan 90
3.5 Creating a Business Plan 96
    3.5.1 Table of Contents 97
    3.5.2 Executive Summary 97
    3.5.3 Description of Your Business 98
    3.5.4 Market Analysis 102
    3.5.5 Marketing Plan 106
    3.5.6 Financial Plan and Statements 109
    3.5.7 Operations Plan 110
    3.5.8 Management and Staffing Plan 112
    3.5.9 Appendices 113

4. Getting Ready to Open 115
4.1 Options for Opening a Bookstore 116
    4.1.1 Buying an Existing Bookstore 116
    4.1.2 Franchising 118
    4.1.3 Opening a New Bookstore 120
4.2 Getting Started 120
    4.2.1 Choosing a Business Name 121
    4.2.2 Your Bookstore's Legal Structure 124
    4.2.3 Business Licenses 128
    4.2.4 Taxes 129
    4.2.5 Insurance 130
4.3 Financing 132
    4.3.1 How Much You'll Need 132
    4.3.2 Preparing to Apply for Funding 137
    4.3.3 Sources of Start-Up Financing 140
    4.3.4 Real-Life Financing Examples 144
4.4 Physical Store 145
    4.4.1 Finding a Space 145
    4.4.2 Signing Your Lease 152

4.4.3 Interior Design 155

4.4.4 Equipment and Supplies 162

4.5 Inventory 170

4.5.1 Buying from Publishers and Wholesalers 171

4.5.2 Buying Remainder Books 176

4.5.3 Buying Used Books 177

4.5.4 Deciding What Books to Buy 181

4.5.5 Buying Sidelines 187

4.5.6 Setting Your Prices 189

4.5.7 Controlling Your Inventory 192

5. Store Operations 195

5.1 Establishing Procedures 195

5.1.1 Developing an Operations Manual 195

5.1.2 Your Employee Handbook 201

5.2 Technology 204

5.2.1 Your Computer System 205

5.2.2 Managing Your Inventory 208

5.2.3 Bookkeeping 209

5.3 Employees 213

5.3.1 Qualities of Great Bookstore Employees 213

5.3.2 Recruiting Staff 215

5.3.3 The Hiring Process 217

5.3.4 New Employees 222

5.4 Opening Day 226

5.5 Marketing Your Bookstore 232

5.5.1 Advertising 232

5.5.2 Events 234

5.5.3 Free Publicity 241

5.5.4 Your Bookstore's Internet Presence 245

5.5.5 Your Email Newsletter 250

5.5.6 Ongoing Marketing 257

5.6 Customer Relations 258

5.6.1 Building Relationships 258

5.6.2 Working with Customers for Feedback 260

6. Staying Competitive **265**

   6.1 Evaluating and Assessing Operations 265

   6.2 Increasing or Decreasing by Category 268

   6.3 Implementing Change 269

7. Resources **271**

   7.1 Professional Associations 271

   7.2 Online Resources 273

1. Introduction

1.1 Welcome to Bookselling

Congratulations on choosing to become a bookstore owner! If you are like most people who decide to open a bookstore, you love books, enjoy reading, and like talking about books with other people. You have dreamed about being your own boss and making your own business decisions. You want to have a career working with what you love — books!

You are about to embark on an amazing adventure. In this guide, the *FabJob Guide to Become a Bookstore Owner*, you will discover how to open and operate your own bookstore. This chapter lays the foundation for the rest of the guide. In the pages that follow you will read about the traits of successful bookstore owners, learn about the job of running a bookstore, and discover some of the benefits of this career.

1.1.1 Traits of Bookstore Owners

While it is impossible to categorize booksellers generally, there are some similarities among bookstore owners. Here are the most significant traits they have in common:

Get Their Hands Dirty

"People think that, in owning a bookstore, they will wear a tweed jacket and smoke a pipe. They don't realize it is a real job. It's a job where you really have to get your hands dirty."

— John King, John K. King Used and Rare Books
Detroit, Michigan

All of the booksellers interviewed for this book are hands-on entrepreneurs involved in the ordinary day-to-day events and operation of their stores. They know where every book is, and they know their customers. Some do everything themselves; others hire competent staff. Still others have figured out over the years the jobs they really don't like or aren't good at and have hired outside sources to help them with various aspects of what they do — like accounting, payroll, or taxes.

Adapt to Change

Booksellers will tell you that the book industry has changed substantially in the last few years, due in large part to technological developments. Booksellers who stay in business and become successful change with the times or with the circumstances that affect them.

Love What They Do

Most bookstore owners make it very clear that they didn't choose to run their own bookstores to become multi-millionaires. Instead, what drives them is a love for what they do. Some of them have been in the book industry for thirty years and others for three, but they all will tell you they have created a place they need and want to be every day. (Some of them say twenty-four hours a day!)

Care About Helping People

Booksellers will tell you that there are many different reasons for a person to walk into a bookstore. It is not always with the intent to buy a book. Sometimes potential customers will simply come in looking for information. They have a topic they want to find out about and they vaguely feel that they can find it in a book. This is when a bookseller becomes an advisor and sometimes even a friend. Helping people solve their problems and find the answers they seek seems to be a continuous thread in what booksellers actually do all day.

A Sense of Community

"Bookselling is as much about creating community as it is about providing books. So if you are a bookseller, and you have an understanding of something your community needs, you deal with that. It doesn't matter whether or not it brings you money — it's just part of the package, it's just how it works."

— Mary Ellen Kavanaugh, My Sisters' Words
Syracuse, New York

Many booksellers say they have created a place that has taken on a life of its own. Their stores are a place of community where people gather and know one another and talk. Many booksellers also feel that they are making an impact on the city or town where they live.

1.1.2 What Bookstore Owners Do

Bookstore owners wear many hats. This section provides a basic overview of the many tasks that bookstore owners are responsible for. As you read through this section, you may find some tasks you would rather not do, either because you don't have expertise in those areas or you simply aren't interested in doing them.

Fortunately, you do not have to do everything yourself. People who are great at what they do know when to get help. For instance, many booksellers choose to have an accountant prepare their business taxes. Many hire web designers to help them with their websites. You could even hire a publicist to help you organize the beginning months of your bookstore's publicity and grand opening gala.

Retail Business Owner

To open your store, you will need to know how to write a business plan, arrange financing, and find a location for your store. Then you will need to know how to operate your store (see "Office Manager" below). Certainly any retail management experience you have had in the past will be helpful, but if you don't have retail management experience, you can learn what you need to know.

Office Manager

As the owner of a bookstore, you will need to know how to run the business side of things. You will need to develop an organized system so you can keep track of your inventory, record sales, pay your bills, and make sure that all aspects of your business are run in an efficient manner. In order to make sure your bookstore is a success you will need to put these important systems into place.

Book Expert

As a bookseller, you are in a unique position of being able to offer your own advice about what books are important to read. While you won't have time to read every book in your store, you must at least have some familiarity with the books you put on your shelves.

You will probably read some of the more important new books you come across each season. You can learn about other books through book reviews, industry publications, and bookseller organizations.

Buyer

You will be responsible for buying the books to stock your shelves. Before you purchase books, you will need to determine the categories of books you will have, and what frontlist and backlist books you want to order.

You will also need to determine what other types of items you want to sell in your store. These items, called sidelines, will vary depending on your personal preferences and bookstore niche. If you have a children's bookstore, you might choose to sell stuffed animals or puzzles or games; if you have a bookstore in a college town you might sell university memorabilia, t-shirts or even dorm supplies.

Sales Professional

When you think of sales, do you think of a cheaply dressed, aggressive salesperson trying to pressure you to buy things that you simply don't want? Do you think of being interrupted at home by telemarketers? Well, sales doesn't have to be a negative thing at all.

The beauty of being a bookseller is that you get a chance to sell something you truly believe in and that you know is a worthwhile thing to own. You get to help people find the best ideas, the most beautiful thoughts, the stories that will change their lives and open their minds. Books provide all of this and more for your customers. The thing to learn about sales is how to find your customers their favorite books — whether or not they have even heard of them yet!

Staffing Expert

Most booksellers don't work alone. As a bookstore owner you will most likely employ a staff of booksellers to work for you. You will need to know what kind of people you want to hire and where to find them.

Then you have to figure out how to train them, how much to pay them, and how to supervise them. You will be the person planning what will happen each day. You will give your employees support and instructions. You will be a leader, a planner, and a visionary.

Event Planner

As a bookseller, you will often be an event planner. The events you plan will help you to develop your bookstore's personality and niche. Customers will come to associate your store with events that were especially memorable to them. It's a great way to bring new business into your store, too.

One wonderful thing you can do as the owner of a bookstore is host author events and book signings. Customers will come from all over and be willing to stand in long lines to get the signature of a well-loved author on a book.

Customer Service Specialist

People remember stores where they feel they have been treated graciously and with respect. Learning to be a customer service expert will increase your bookstore's sales and improve your store's reputation. People will remember your bookstore as "the place where they are nice to people."

Quiz: Do You Have an Aptitude for Bookselling?

In order to help you see if your personality traits and attitudes are similar to other booksellers, I asked a number of booksellers to describe "book people." This quiz will help you measure your own traits against those that booksellers deem as important.

Directions: Decide how strongly you feel about the following statements. For each one, pick the answer that fits the best:

	Strongly Disagree		Neutral		Strongly Agree
I like people.	1	2	3	4	5
I am an extrovert.	1	2	3	4	5
I enjoy using my creativity.	1	2	3	4	5
I am not afraid to work hard.	1	2	3	4	5
I am organized.	1	2	3	4	5
I pay attention to detail.	1	2	3	4	5
I have a retail background.	1	2	3	4	5
I love to read.	1	2	3	4	5
I am a problem solver.	1	2	3	4	5
People say I am a good listener.	1	2	3	4	5
I like people.	1	2	3	4	5
I like helping people get answers.	1	2	3	4	5
I care about people and their needs.	1	2	3	4	5
I enjoy research.	1	2	3	4	5
I have a lot of energy.	1	2	3	4	5
I enjoy meeting new people.	1	2	3	4	5
I like to travel.	1	2	3	4	5
I have management experience.	1	2	3	4	5
I'm not afraid to delegate.	1	2	3	4	5
I get committed to things I feel passionately about.	1	2	3	4	5
I love to try new things.	1	2	3	4	5

How Did You Score?

As you determined your level of agreement with the statements above, you probably noticed that you either agreed or strongly agreed with many of them.

Booksellers, as well as small business owners and entrepreneurs, share many of the traits represented by the statements above. The more questions you agreed with (i.e. answered with either a 4 or a 5), the more qualities you share with the actual booksellers whose remarks were taken from interviews to create this test.

While some of these qualities are obviously useful to a bookseller (such as enjoying meeting people, love of reading, and retail experience), later in this guide you will discover how the other traits listed above are valuable for a bookseller to have. For example, if you like to travel, you will be more likely to enjoy attending trade shows for the book industry.

When determining your results, a neutral answer, or one in which you disagree or strongly disagree, doesn't necessarily mean that bookselling isn't for you. What it does mean is that there are some tasks involved with bookselling, or some character traits that many booksellers share, that might not be your strong point.

This is an indication that you may need training in an area (like retail or management experience) or that you might want to delegate certain tasks or parts of your bookselling business to others — either staff you hire or outside experts.

All in all, this exercise is a success if it helps you to look clearly at those things that you answered with a neutral or negative response to determine how you will best handle them to achieve the greatest overall success in your own bookstore.

1.1.3 Benefits of This Career

As you saw from the "job description" above, being a bookseller gives you the opportunity to enjoy varied and challenging work. Booksellers often remark about how they absolutely never get bored — not even for a second. Here are some of the other benefits that bookstore owners enjoy:

Be Around Books

In a typical day you will think about, read, discuss, critique, recommend, buy and sell books. You will have a chance to find out what books are new and exciting, and learn about the greatest new authors on the scene. You will get to remember books that are old favorites and not-to-be missed classics. You will be able to stock your shelves with books that you feel really matter.

Focus on What You Love

As a bookseller, you can focus on a subject area or topic you really love. Do you enjoy children's books? You can open a children's bookstore. Do you love travel? A travel bookstore might be perfect for you. What about old and rare books? Why not open an antiquarian bookstore? Whatever drives your love of books – your passion – can come into play in your own bookstore.

Control Your Career

Owning a bookstore is an excellent way to control how and when and where you make a living.

Have you always wanted to make your own hours, and decide when and how to work? As a bookstore owner, you will be able to do just that. Do you want to open early for people on their way to the office? You can. Do you want to have late weekend hours so customers make your bookstore the after-hours hangout? It's up to you.

You will have the freedom to make your own decisions and express your own creative spirit. The sky is the limit when you own your own bookstore — if you have an idea, you can try it.

Express Your Opinion

Do you enjoy talking with other people about books? Can you explain why a certain book is a good book and why it might be useful or enjoyable to someone else? Your opinion about books will matter in your store — and you are the expert.

Make a Difference

There is nothing quite like the satisfaction of helping people get what they need. You will have a chance to get to know your customers and to help them choose books that really make a difference in their lives. Some bookstore owners feel that this is the single most gratifying part about being a bookseller.

Create Exciting Events and Meet Famous Authors

One wonderful aspect of owning your own bookstore is that you suddenly have your own venue. You can give parties, and have authors come to your store for book signings and other events. You can host activities that will put you on the map in your town or city.

Be a Community Leader

As a bookstore owner, you can become a vital part of the business community. As you make contacts in your community, you can enjoy a good public reputation. Your bookstore might even become a must-see for tourists, or a town institution that no one could ever imagine living without.

If you are excited about the points above and the prospect of making these things real in your own life, you have taken the first step to becoming a bookstore owner.

1.2 Inside This Guide

This book was written to help you achieve your dream of owning your own bookstore. In it you will find everything from the basics to the information that all industry insiders know.

If you have never owned your own business, it is a good idea to read the book from beginning to end and follow the instructions step-by-step. If you have experience with your own business, you may want to read through the Table of Contents and select the sections you feel will be the most helpful to you.

Chapter 2 (Learning the Business) will give you an insider's view of the book industry. You'll see how a book gets from the writer to the reader, discover different book categories and learn about types of bookstores. The chapter concludes with additional ways for you to develop your knowledge and skills.

Chapter 3 (Planning for Your Bookstore) can help you get greater clarity on what you want in your own bookstore. You will visualize your dream bookstore in every detail, and then get some practical planning tools to move from the idea stage to making your bookstore a reality.

In Chapter 4 (Getting Ready to Open) you will learn how to set up your bookstore, step-by-step. This chapter will help you decide whether to buy an existing store or open a new one, and what kind of funding you will need. You will also get pointers on organizing and arranging the actual interior of your store and building an inventory of books.

Chapter 5 (Store Operations) takes you into the day-to-day challenge of running your bookstore once it's open. It covers your daily routine, working with staff and customers, marketing, accounting, and holding events.

Chapter 6 (Staying Competitive) offers advice to help your bookstore grow and make positive changes as you go along. Finally, chapter 7 gives you important industry resources and links to other information that will help you get started.

By following the steps in this guide, you will be well on your way to living your dream — owning your own bookstore!

2. Learning The Business

As you look at books on bookstore shelves, it is amazing to ponder how much creativity, hard work, effort, planning, coordination, and organization takes place to get books from the writer to the reader. After reading this chapter, you'll understand more about how it all happens.

This chapter is like an introductory course in bookselling. It covers the following essentials that every bookstore owner should understand:

- Book industry terminology

- How books get from the writer's hands to the customer's hands

- How to tell one end of a book from another

- How books are organized once they actually get to a bookstore

- Types of bookstores and booksellers

In addition to a good overview of bookselling, you will discover a variety of resources and techniques to learn even more about the industry and prepare yourself for this rewarding career.

2.1 The Language of Bookselling

This section explains the terminology you will need to know as a bookseller.

We wanted to make this potentially mundane task of learning industry lingo a little more lively. Considering that most future bookstore owners love words, we have created a crossword puzzle that will satisfy your love of words and help you master the fundamental technical terms simultaneously.

The terms are defined throughout this chapter — but try doing the puzzle first to see how much you already know!

Bookstore Terms Crossword Puzzle

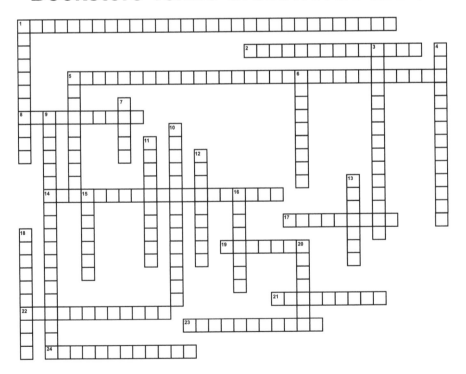

Across

1 The national organization for booksellers.

2 A display of books placed in a bookstore to draw special attention.

5 The national association for Canadian booksellers.

8 A copy of a book given to a reviewer or bookseller to read ahead of its release date.

14 A smaller paperback, usually a best-seller, printed on inexpensive paper designed to sell in racks in stores.

17 New book releases from publishers expected to be successful sellers.

19 The page or pages after the front free-endpaper.

21 A person who makes a living buying valuable used books and selling them again.

22 The place in a bookstore where customers make purchases.

23 The first date a new book can be placed on retail shelves.

24 Fiction based on a specific type like romance, science fiction or mystery.

Down

1 Old and rare books.

3 POP.

4 The approximately 40% discount that booksellers get from publishers when purchasing books.

5 The designated groupings of books that are placed together by subject.

6 Non-book items sold in bookstores.

7 The hard edge of the book that covers the place where the pages of the book are bound.

9 The overall manner a bookseller displays books in a store to attract sales.

10 Paperback books made with good quality paper that come in a variety of sizes.

11 A book distributor that buys from publishers and sells to booksellers.

12 Advertising money to assist a bookseller in selling a book from a publisher.

13 New book releases from publishers not expected to be best-sellers

15 A midlist book that suddenly takes off in sales.

16 Books that are no longer new but determined to sell well.

18 The protective cover on a new hard cover book.

20 The front-cover-out placement of a book on a shelf.

Crossword Puzzle Answers

```
A M E R I C A N B O O K S E L L E R S A S S O C I A T I O N
N                                     F E A T U R E D I S P L A Y   V
T                                                       O           E
I       C A N A D I A N B O O K S E L L E R S A S S O C I A T I O N
Q       A               S               I           N           D
U       T                               D           T           O
A   R E V I E W C O P Y                 E           O           R
R   I   G           I           T       L           F           D
I   S   O       N   W   R       I       P           I           I
A   U   R       E   H   A   C   N       U           S           S
N   A   I           O   D   O   E       R           M   C       C
    A   L           L   E   O   S       C           I   H       O
    L   E           L           O               M   D   A       U
    M A S S M A R K E T P A P E R B A C K       I   D   N       N
    E   L           S   A   M   A       F R O N T L I S T       T
    R   E           A   P   O   C           I   S   E
    C   P           L   E   N   K       F L Y L E A F
  D C   E           E   R   E   B Y Y       I   S
  U H   E           R   B   E   Y           S   T
  S A   R               A                   T
  T N                   C
  J D                   K               B O O K S C O U T
  A I                                   U
  C A S H W R A P A R E A       L A Y D O W N D A T E
  K N
  E N
  T G E N R E F I C T I O N
```

Some book industry words included in the puzzle are defined here:

- A *display area* is a special display that highlights a specific book or series of books.

- *Sections* or *categories* are the designated groupings of books that are placed together by subject.

- A *floor display* is a type of *display pack* — that is, a cardboard or other type of display that publishers sometimes send along with certain books to draw attention to them.

- A *feature display* is a display of books that the bookstore owner is trying to draw attention to by special placement in the store.

- *Visual merchandising* is the overall technique by which a bookstore owner sets up a display to best highlight books in the store.

- The *cash-wrap area* is the place in a bookstore where customers buy their books.

- A *POP* or *point of purchase display* is a display created at the cash-wrap area to sell something — whether a book or s*ideline.*

2.2 The Book Industry

2.2.1 Who's Who in the Book Industry

When you become a bookseller, all of the books on the shelves of your store will be there because of an intricate network of hard working book industry professionals. Listed below are brief descriptions of the jobs these book industry professionals do that make bookselling not only a possibility, but also a reality.

The Writers

Writers are the people who have the daunting task of creating the text of the books you will sell in your store. Without writers there would be no book industry. Writers work to put the perfect words on paper to convey their ideas. They research and write, and rewrite and rewrite again, to complete manuscripts they think are ready to submit.

With any luck, you may get to meet a few of them and have them come to your store to meet your customers at book signings and other events you dream up.

The Literary Agents

Literary agents are the official go-betweens who connect talented writers with publishers who will publish their books. In today's publishing industry, a lot of writers work without agents and forge bravely ahead making their own book deals.

There are different schools of thought about this. On one hand, writers working without agents make all of the money they contract for themselves — there is no one with whom they agree to split the pie. On the other hand, many writers are purely creative types who often don't have the business acumen to sell themselves and cut fantastic, lucrative deals.

Great literary agents are both enthusiastic cheerleaders and savvy dealmakers for writers.

The Publishers

It is the job of publishers to decide what kind of books consumers want from season to season and put them in print. Most publishers have a specific subject area or category that they prefer to publish.

Some publishers are very small, and some are considered independent publishers. Others are gigantic houses full of hundreds of people, often made larger by many recent acquisitions of smaller publishing houses.

An industry mainstay – a book called Literary Market Place – lists all of the publishers in the industry, gives relevant details about the types of books they publish, and lists the number of titles they publish annually. By going to **www.literarymarketplace.com** and filling out a free registration form, you can browse their online database of publishers. However, you will have to pay a subscription fee ($399/year or $19.95/week) if you wish to view more detailed information about each publisher.

The Acquisitions Editors

These talented editors work for publishers and make the initial decisions about which writers and which manuscripts should be considered for publication. Some acquisitions editors work off hot lists — lists of potential book subjects for which a publisher is actively looking for submissions. Other acquisition editors ask for authors to submit proposals for books based on defined subject areas or even for an existing line of books that the house already publishes.

In order to get published, writers must connect with acquisitions editors and convince them that their books or book ideas are worthy enough to pass along to an editorial board.

The Editorial Boards

Editorial boards are composed of groups of editors in any publishing house who work as a team to decide which book manuscripts, or proposals for book manuscripts, they are going to accept. These groups of editors work together to read the work of writers and decide which books will be successful. Often, the editorial team will meet and deliberate for months at a time before deciding to offer a book contract to a new writer.

The Managing Editors

Managing editors, who are often also successful writers, turn the manuscripts that the writers submit into publishing gold. It is the responsibility of managing editors to work closely with writers to get manuscripts completely ready for publication. Managing editors not only have to have superb writing skills, but also must be able to communicate effectively, schedule realistically, and get everyone involved in the editing process to, literally, stay on the same page.

The Proofreaders

Proofreaders are the people who know language. They are the grammar and punctuation wordsmiths who take a manuscript in hand and make sure that there are no errors in syntax. Without these very talented and precise masters of the English language, books would have errors. And one all-important thing that everyone in this industry agrees upon is that words are all important — and they need to be put together with elegance and precision.

The Printers

Once manuscripts have been accepted and revised by publishing house editors, they are ready to go to the printer. These printers are far more specialized than corner copy stores where you get your copies made — these are printing companies that specialize in the printing of books. This special part of the book industry is really its own world, complete with its own jargon. You really don't need to have expert knowledge of the printing industry as a bookseller, but you will need to be able to identify the basic parts of a book. We will cover this more in depth in section 2.3.1.

The Publisher's Sales Representatives

Sometimes called sales reps, these are the people from a publishing house who work with you directly in your effort to purchase books for your bookstore. Based on the size of your store, your location, and the location and size of the publisher, sales reps may come to see you in person, or they may develop a relationship with you over the phone as you repeatedly order books.

The Wholesalers

Wholesalers buy books from a variety of publishers and sell them to booksellers. By using a wholesaler to purchase books, you can often find most of the books you want at one time with one phone call.

However, the books from wholesalers will generally be the staples of your stock. New books that are yet to be released and that are potentially this season's best-sellers will come directly from the publishers. As a bookseller, you will generally have a buying relationship with several wholesalers and a number of publishers.

The Book Critics

Book critics often set the tone for whether or not new books become hits. In fact, it has been proven again and again that the popular press and media can take a book over the top. Many potential customers read the New York Times Book Review and the Washington Post Book World, and purchase – or at least look at – books based on reviewers' recommendations.

- *The New York Times Book Review*
  www.nytimes.com/pages/books/review/index.html

- *The Washington Post Book World*
  www.washingtonpost.com/wp-dyn/print/sunday/bookworld

2.2.2 The Life Cycle of a Book

Before you begin the "nuts and bolts" of planning for your own bookstore, it is important to understand some of the basics about the industry. As you read the job titles in the previous section, you probably got the sense that many people in many different jobs take a book from the idea in an author's head to the end result of a bookstore customer's purchase.

So how does a book get on your new bookstore's shelves? How does it move from idea stage to published form? What does a publisher do with it? How is it marketed? How is it sold? Let's follow a book from its moment of inception to the moment a customer pays for it at the counter of your new bookstore.

From the Writer to the Publisher

Inspiration

To begin with, the writer must have an idea, or an inspiration about what to write. Sometimes writers get the ideas themselves, or sometimes, if they have been working with acquisition editors long enough and have established relationships, editors will help writers pick a topic or an idea to write about.

Expressing Inspiration and Selling Ideas

After the writer decides upon an idea, they must create a proposal to sell the idea to a publisher. Even from the idea stage, a book is being sold. An effective proposal can secure the writer a contract and an advance — prepayment to the author against future royalties for a book. The royalties for a book are based on a percentage of the sales.

Packaging Ideas as Books

Once a contract is signed, and the author writes and submits a book, the publisher's work begins. Now the editors assigned to the book project must make sure it is packaged in a way that fits the publisher's brand, and contains the content and reflects the sort of image the publisher wants to associate with the publishing house.

All the way through this process, publishers know what kind of books sell for them and how they must look and read.

From The Publisher to the Bookseller

Even before the book is written, publishers are concentrating on creating a marketing strategy that will help them sell a book. At the publisher's level, the name of the game is selling books, and publishers do this several ways.

For the most part, publishers sell their books to two markets — booksellers and wholesalers. One way to do this includes giving review copies or *advanced reading copies* (also called ARCs) to book reviewers and booksellers in hope of generating a positive "buzz."

TIP: Review copies or advanced reading copies are copies of books given to reviewers or booksellers before a book is published in the publisher's effort to generate good reviews and sell more books.

Another trick used by publishers is to decide what kind of display packs or feature displays they will provide with a book to attract attention to it once it's in the bookstore.

TIP: *Display packs* are displays, often made out of cardboard, that are sent from a publisher with an order of books. They might sit on a counter top or other display area, and are designed to draw attention to a book.

Additional ways that publishers market books include:

- Television, radio, and print advertising

- Selling an upcoming book through their catalogs to booksellers, libraries, or other interested potential buyers

- Selling upcoming books at regional, national, and international trade shows aimed at booksellers

- Offering booksellers "co-op" money to sell a book — that is, advertising money that a bookseller can use to promote a book in their store

- Asking an author to go on a book tour to promote their book at various book signings around the country

- Asking an author to be interviewed by media about their book

The publisher must cooperate with the bookseller in order to ultimately have their books reach a public market. Publishers' work in selling books all happens before a book's laydown date.

TIP: A book's *laydown date* is set by the publisher and is the first day a retailer can display a new book. This laydown date becomes especially anticipated and important in the case of giant titles like new Harry Potter releases.

From the Bookseller to the Customer

Before you have a single book on the shelves of your new bookstore, you will have to order it. You will work with publishers and wholesalers to buy the books you want.

Buying From Publishers

Establishing working relationships with a number of publishers will be the first step. Depending upon the size and location of your bookstore, publishers will either send a sales rep to you, or you will work with one over the phone.

Frontlist, Midlist, and Backlist Books

To begin with, you might view publishers' catalogs or read review or advanced reading copies of books to determine which books you want to order. You will want to order a good mix of frontlist, midlist and backlist books.

Frontlist books have not yet been released by a publisher and are new in any given book season. Publishers usually release books in two and occasionally three seasons — fall, spring, and sometimes summer.

Books that are still new, but that will probably not be best-sellers, are called *midlist* books. Books that have been out for a while, but that are still good sellers, are called *backlist* books.

Occasionally a book that is considered a midlist book may suddenly take off and become popular, even a best-seller. When this happens, it is referred to in the industry as a *sleeper*.

Overstocks and Remainder Books

Many times publishers print too many copies of a certain book. If they feel they will not be able to sell it, they will reduce the price and call it an *overstock* or *remainder* book. It is important to ask your sales rep about these books because you can get them at a greatly reduced price.

Buying From Wholesalers

Wholesalers are another place to get midlist and backlist books, as well as remainders and overstocks. One advantage of buying from wholesalers is that they generally buy from many different publishers, so they are a convenient way for new booksellers to stock their stores.

Many times a wholesaler's rep can give you a list of what books are best to stock for your backlist titles, and they will generally try to help you as much as they can. Naturally, this is a two-way street. If they can assist you with what to buy, you may be able to buy more. It is very important to go into this buying situation knowing and sticking to the budget you have determined for your book inventory.

After the Order and to Your Bookshelves

As you are reviewing your book orders, there are a number of things to pay attention to. You will notice that you have purchased books at what is called a *vendor's discount*. Normally this discount is around 40 percent off the retail price, but if it is less, it is referred to as a *short discount*. Section 4.5 has more information about how to buy books for your bookstore.

Into the Customer's Hands

After you open your doors, customers will stroll through your display areas. Hopefully they will be attracted by your imaginative visual merchandising, your floor and feature displays, and attractively displayed new and interesting books placed face-out so titles can be easily seen.

Eventually, the customers will make their way to your cashier's area to pay for their purchases. Here they might see a *point-of-purchase* (POP) display that entices them to buy yet another book.

Sometimes a potential customer will come in wanting a specific book that you don't have. You can special order this book for them.

Also, in order to minimize the amount of money needed to put books on shelves, some booksellers do what is called *just-in-time* (JIT) ordering, which means they order books from wholesalers in less quantity but more frequently.

2.3 The Books

"A book is an asset in our society, a treasure, a thing to respect and behold; the adventure in a dull life; the awe for another time and place; tons of knowledge; and so much more than I can explain."

— Pat Tegtmeier, A Novel View
Anchorage, Alaska

2.3.1 Parts of a Book

They say, "You can't tell a book by its cover," but perhaps you can. There are many things you can find out about books by looking at them. And, as a bookseller, you will want to be able to examine the books you buy carefully to check their condition, and – in the case of first editions, used books, old books, and rare books – their worth.

To assist you in learning about books, get a book that you can hold in your hand and examine as you read the following section.

Hardcover or Paperback

Probably the easiest thing to determine is whether you are holding a hardcover book or a paperback book. A *hardcover book* has a board or hard cover and a *paperback book* has a cover made of some kind of laminated heavy paper. Most booksellers sell both types of books in their stores.

Mass-Market or Trade Paperback

A *mass-market paperback* is the type of paperback you might find in your supermarket in the book section, near the magazines in racks. This type of book is smaller than trade paperbacks and printed on rather inexpensive paper. Mass-market paperbacks include the top ten best-selling new novels.

A *trade paperback* is usually larger, the type of paperback book you might find in a regular bookstore. Trade paperbacks are made with a higher quality paper than mass market paperbacks and come in a variety of sizes.

The Dust Jacket

A completely self-explanatory name, the *dust jacket* is the printed jacket that accompanies a new hardcover book to protect it. One interesting thing about a dust jacket is that its intact presence greatly increases the value of a modern first edition or an old book. Naturally, if you are going to buy used books as part of your stock, you will want to be on the lookout for dust jackets as you purchase books.

The Spine and Label

The *spine* is the hard edge of the book that covers the place where its pages are bound. The spine in a book basically provides the mechanism to hold it together.

It is also used for identification purposes. Spines of books will usually give you the title of the book, the publisher, and the name of the author. Naturally, this is vital for anyone shelving books because it allows you to see the title of each book. This identification on the spine of the book is called the *label*.

The Endpaper and the Pastedown

The endpapers help to hold the pages of the book in place. An endpaper is made up of two components, the pastedown and the free-endpaper. When you open a book's cover, the first page you come to is the *endpaper*. The page on the left side is glued to the cover and is called the *pastedown*. The page on the right side is the *front free-endpaper*.

You will find another endpaper in the back of the book that attaches the back right cover of the book to the rest of the pages. Again, the page that's glued to the back cover is called the pastedown and the other side is called the *back free-endpaper*.

The Flyleaf

After you turn the page that is called the front free-endpaper, you will see at least one and sometimes several blank pages. These are called the *flyleaf*. Sometimes one of these pages will have just the title of the book without any other information. This is still considered a flyleaf.

The Title Page

Another fairly self-explanatory part of the book is the title page. On the *title page* you will find the title of the book, the author's name and the name of the publisher.

The Copyright Page

The *copyright page* lists the book's copyright information, Library of Congress information, ISBN number, and any legal disclaimers or other pertinent legal information. It also lists the author (last name first), the publisher, and the date the book was published. Additionally, you can find out where the book was printed, as well as information that the publisher uses to denote the edition of the book.

The Signatures

The signatures of a book have nothing to do with an author's signature. *Signatures* are the blocks of pages that, when put together, make up the pages of text in a book. Printers organize books by groups of pages called signatures, which consist of a specified number of printed pages that are formed by folding and binding large sheets of paper into the number of pages in a signature.

When an author, editor, or publisher is determining the number of pages that a new book will have, they must make sure that the final number of pages is equal to the number of pages contained in the signatures.

The Text Block

The *text block* makes up the pages of text in a book. It is formed when all of the signatures are bound into book form. To view a list of more definitions, visit **www.alibris.com/glossary/glossary.cfm**.

2.3.2 Book Categories

To assist customers in finding the right books, booksellers arrange them by category. There are two major categories of books — fiction and non-fiction. Within these categories are many subcategories.

Book Categories

Fiction

Commercial Fiction

- Paperback fiction
- Best-sellers
- New hardcover books
- New paperback books

Contemporary Fiction

- General fiction
- Romance
- Mysteries and thrillers
- Science fiction and fantasy
- Westerns
- Horror

Poetry and Drama

- Poetry collections
- Poetry anthologies
- Plays
- Screenplays
- Film and theater biographies

Classic Fiction

- Literary anthologies
- Literary fiction
- Classic works by literary masters

Nonfiction

- General nonfiction
- History and biography
- Personal development
- Health and fitness
- Reference
- Art
- Technology and computers
- Architecture
- "Niche" books (*e.g.* gay and lesbian nonfiction)
- Spirituality
- Theater and film
- Science
- Crafts
- Cookbooks
- Textbooks
- Business and money management
- Travel

Special Areas

- Foreign language books
- Humor, comics and graphic novels
- DVDs
- Audio books (divided by relevant categories)
- Music, musical scores, books about music

Children's Books

Children's Fiction

- Picture books
- Chapter books
- Series books
- Classics
- Young Adult fiction
- Humor and comics

Children's Nonfiction

- General nonfiction
- History and Biography
- Science
- Crafts
- How-to
- Cooking
- Sports

Special Children's Areas

- Children's DVDs
- Children's music
- Toys
- Games
- Book and toy combinations
- Books and craft kit combinations
- Foreign language books

Most bookstores try to have their books arranged logically so that customers who are interested in one kind of book will find themselves moving through that category right through to something else close enough in content to grab their interest. It's a good idea to visit several bookstores to browse the category sections so you see how they have them set up. Section 2.5 has tips on how to gather information about how bookstores operate.

2.4 The Bookstores

Bookstores come in all shapes and sizes. From the tiniest independent bookstore to the largest superstore, there are many ways to sell books. Being an independent bookseller allows you the freedom of creating your own special world; a place that you feel expresses your passion for books.

As a new bookseller, you should be familiar with the many types of booksellers in the book industry today. You should also be familiar with the different kinds of independent bookstores, including:

- New bookstores

- Used bookstores

- Combination bookstores

- Antiquarian or old and rare bookstores

Following is a more complete explanation of the various types of bookstores in the industry today, and the advantages about each of the various types of independent bookstores.

2.4.1 Where Books Are Sold

To begin our overview, let's look briefly at the major kinds of bookstores.

The Independent Bookstore

"Independent bookstores have knowledge, passion, character, and community."

— Oren J. Teicher, CEO
American Booksellers Association

Independent bookstores are bookstores owned by individual business owners, partners, and smaller companies. As a bookseller, this is the type of bookstore you will own unless you have the financial backing of a major corporation behind you, or are one of those self-made business tycoons who start from nothing and create empires.

If what you want is a small kingdom – a place where you can help your "subjects" find the subjects they are interested in – then you will be an independent bookstore owner.

Unlike chain or superstore bookstores, independent bookstores are in practically every city in the United States and in Canada, and they come in all specialties or niches. There are mystery bookstores, religious bookstores, and bookstores designed for teachers and science fiction enthusiasts. There are bookstores devoted purely to plays, feminism, and business. There are college bookstores, and of course bookstores devoted completely to children's books.

An independent bookseller has the luxury of selling the type of books they want to sell. As an independent bookseller you can sell all new books, all used books, a combination of both, or even extremely rare and collectible books. It is possible to have a bookstore that sells a wide variety of different categories of books, or to pick a specific genre or specialty and focus on that. Independent booksellers love the freedom their stores provide them — the freedom to choose.

Independent booksellers will always be able to do something that the superstore can't — keep the heart and soul of books available to customers. Independent bookstores are where the passionate love affair with the written word will always exist. Books are personal — they are worlds to be enjoyed, shared, and reveled in. No giant supermarket of books will ever top a one-on-one conversation that a happy customer shares with a knowledgeable and interested bookseller about the thing they are both passionate about.

The "Competition"

It is important for you to know your competition. Competition might be other independent bookstores, super-stores or chain stores, Internet bookstores, discount stores, price clubs, or even grocery stores.

The Superstore

Just like it sounds, the superstores are the big ones — think Borders or Barnes and Noble. These are the giant supermarkets of books. Some independent booksellers fear them because they feel that they will "eat them up."

However, if you can strategically place and market your independent store, you don't need to fear these stores. You can simply consider them the generic bookstores for the masses.

The Internet Bookstore

Amazon.com started it, and now others have followed in their footsteps. Amazon.com could be considered the superstore of Internet books with BarnesandNoble.com providing its biggest competition. But Amazon is unique because it does not have a physical presence or what is known as a "brick and mortar" store.

Many independent bookstore owners feel that Internet bookstores are hurting their businesses, but with excellent programs like the American Bookseller Association's BookSense, you can get help creating a viable Internet presence for your new bookstore and get in on the Internet trade competition. (See section 5.5.4 for more information on BookSense).

Other Places that Sell Books

If you have been out to shop lately you have probably noticed that it's not only bookstores that carry books these days. Supermarkets, department stores, warehouse stores and even office supply stores carry books.

As you begin to think about what businesses your own store might be competing with, don't forget to find out about all of the businesses in the surrounding area that sell books. The answer to this question can be surprising!

2.4.2 Types of Independent Bookstores

New Bookstores

New books. Brand new, off the shelf, never-been-opened books. For many booksellers, and customers alike, opening a book for the first time is still a thrill. The way a book opens for the first time when no other person has ever opened it is something many people who love to read enjoy experiencing. It is as if the book is especially for them and they are experiencing the magic of it for the first time. New books are exciting.

Is it For You?

If you love to read the New York Times Book Review, you eagerly antici-pate the new writing of favorite authors, and you are always on the look-out for new up-and-coming writers to hit the scene, a bookstore that sells new books may be perfect for you.

Selling New Books

When you run a bookstore that sells new books, you will have to charge the prices that publishers decide upon. Unlike used book sales, where you have more control over sales margins, you have a fixed percentage of profit in new book sales. This is why many new booksellers also fea-ture sidelines (other merchandise that they sell in their stores) or cafés to increase overall profit margin.

When selling new books, you will have the opportunity to work with pub-lishers using co-op money and take advantage of any existing publicity they have generated about new releases. You should talk in depth with the sales rep from each publisher and wholesaler about how to best market the books and whether they have any programs to help you sell.

Being Aware and Informed About New Releases

Also, as a new bookseller, you will need to be aware of new books and upcoming releases. You will need to read reviews, attend trade shows, and talk to others in the industry to make sure you are aware of what books will be hot for any coming release season. An excellent way to do this is to get advanced reading copies from publishers' sales reps and review publishers' catalogs for each new season.

Carefully Assessing Your Market and Your Customers

Just like with any other retail product, when selling new books you will need to be very aware of your market and the customers you are hoping to attract. You will need to make sure you carry the books your custom-ers want and that you pursue the advertising that will attract customers who will buy the kind of books your bookstore carries. Like any other kind of retail store, it is a give and take between what you want to sell and what customers want to buy.

Used Bookstores

"Where do homeless books go? Often, in the dumpster. I believe my bookstore is akin to an adoption agency for homeless books, matching them up with caring readers of all ages. And, oh the readers! So dedicated to reading, and often devoted to specific authors. Our readers are our major source of books, when they bring them to us for consideration in the store. The books are accepted if we believe they are saleable, clean and undamaged, if they don't duplicate what we already have, and if we have room for them."

— Pat Tegtmeier, A Novel View
Anchorage, Alaska

Used books are interesting. You never know what book you will find when you enter a used bookstore. And every book you open has an interesting story to tell. Each used book you look at has been on a journey, and has been read and owned by someone else. It's sometimes as fascinating to contemplate the journey of a used book as it is to read it. Many booksellers who love used books feel like their world is constantly full of surprises and amazing finds.

Is it For You?

Selling used books may be for you if:

- You have always loved to haunt used bookstores

- You are always looking for authors you may have missed along your search

- A discovery of a favorite author's book you have somehow missed over the years is like finding an old friend

The World of Used Book Sales

When you run a used bookstore you have a lot of options about the books you sell. Most importantly, you have control of the prices you charge. And while you make about a 40 percent profit in new book sales, you can often find old books very inexpensively and sell them for quite a bit more — especially when they are valuable.

Where Used Bookstores Get Stock

Some used bookstores feature what are called "old and rare" books, mostly aimed at collectors. However, most used bookstores range from a disorderly mishmash of all kinds of books to a highly-ordered store filled with specific categories of well-cared-for books.

As a used bookseller you can find your stock from many places. Some used booksellers travel to book fairs and various sales around the country where books are sometimes for sale by the inch or even by the pound. Other used booksellers buy books directly from their own customers. Still others buy from estate sales, library sales, or even garage sales. Still others buy from book scouts — people who travel around the country (and around the Internet) in an effort to find important used books.

Doing Your Homework and Learning the Business

Used booksellers have a good understanding of literature. Most of them are well-read and use their general knowledge of books to help them not only find books to sell, but help customers find what they want. And while it is completely impossible to know everything about every book, it definitely helps if you personally love used books and read them.

Carefully Assessing Your Market and Your Customers

As you start to get to know your customers, it is important to talk to them. Finding out what books they love, what authors they collect, and where else they look for used books can be infinitely helpful to you as a used bookseller. Let customers fill out "wish lists" of books that they would love to own if you find them. Doing this can help you build your business, introduce you to authors you are unaware of that you will want to be on the lookout for, and create a buzz for your store.

Combination Bookstores

"I have found over the years that books change people's lives. Whether new books or old, I couldn't sell anything else. Bookstores are the pivot points for relationships, for building community, for forming a soul for the community. The customer and staff feed each other and the world at large through the written word."

> — Gayle Shanks, Changing Hands Bookstore
> Tempe, Arizona

Some independent bookstore owners prefer the best of both worlds and choose to sell both new and used books. One reason this is smart is because some customers shop for only the newest and latest things, best-sellers, and what Oprah talked about this week, while others shop for books based on topics that interest them and prefer them at a reduced price.

The profit margin on used books can be quite high, while the profit margin for new books and best-sellers is smaller and set by publishers. In a combination store there is usually something for everyone.

Is it For You?

If you love new and used books, and have a great deal of energy, commitment and capacity to learn, owning a combination bookstore may be perfect for you. With an open mind and some time to learn both ends of the industry, you will become a whiz at stocking and selling new books, and will get to know how the used book business works.

Getting Comfortable with it All

As you go along learning to sell both new and used books, you may find that the best way to do it is to hire some staff, or work with a partner with whom you can divvy up some of the responsibilities and chores of running a business that caters to both customers who love new books and those who love used books. You will also find that the diverse selection you have in your store will make it possible for more customers to find what they want — and at a variety of prices.

By being able to control your prices on the used end of things you will be able to add to your profits without sacrificing the new books and the readership that prefers them.

Carefully Assessing Your Market and Your Customers

As a bookseller who sells both new and used books, you will have a special challenge to present the wide option of buying choices to your potential customers. Also, based on the variety of your bookstore, you will have a wider customer base to draw from.

It will be important to talk to customers and perhaps even keep track of the books that customers buy to track which advertising choices bring in which customers. With time you will get a chance to know your customers, understand how you are attracting them, and determine your best sources for advertising.

Antiquarian Bookstores

"Just because a book is old it doesn't make it valuable, and just because a book is recent it doesn't make it valueless."

— Al Navis, Almark and Company, Booksellers
Ontario, Canada

Old and rare books are one of the most fascinating parts of the bookselling industry. Booksellers involved in the buying and selling of old and rare books are more than booksellers — they are collectors and often book historians. This specialized world has a different set of rules and different requirements than other areas of bookselling. And those involved in the old and rare book business take it very seriously.

Antiquarian book dealers work mostly with collectors. Some don't even keep regular office or store hours. Some meet with collectors by appointment; others have made the Internet their base of operations and have a physical warehouse instead of a storefront location.

Is it For You?

If you love research, enjoy the minutiae of painstakingly finding out all you can about a certain author, book, or series of books, and you can imagine yourself spending hours of time on the Internet hunting for, researching, buying and selling collectible books, then perhaps an antiquarian bookstore is right for you.

A Diverse International Industry

More so than most other parts of the book industry, the antiquarian book industry really works in an international marketplace. Dealers from all over the world interact and come together in organizations like The International League of Antiquarian Booksellers (**www.ilab-lila.com**).

In order to become a part of this organization, an antiquarian bookseller must first join their national organization. The process is a complicated one, requiring that you first find four sponsors who are already part of the organization. These sponsors then make sure that your rare book business meets the criteria set forth by the organization. In essence, membership is earned and selective. However, if you wish to be an antiquarian bookseller, membership in these prestigious organizations is an excellent idea and an important goal.

Carefully Assessing Your Market and Your Customers

The antiquarian market is something you can research and access over the Internet. There are several key sites that will allow you to access the world of rare book traders and see what they are trading at any given point. It is important for you, as an antiquarian bookseller, to carefully learn and research your part of the industry. And luckily, much of this can be done online, at sites such as these:

- *Advanced Book Exchange (ABE)*
  www.abebooks.com

- *Association of College and Research Libraries FAQ*
  www.rbms.nd.edu/yob.html

Specialty and Niche Bookstores

"We have found that successful independent stores have a niche and understand their locality instead of trying to do everything for everyone."

— Suzanne Brooks, President
Canadian Booksellers Association

Just as you have seen that there are several different types of bookstores you can own, there are also a variety of specialties or niches that you can focus on.

One of the most attractive things about owning your own bookstore is that you can sell books that you feel are important and go after the share of the market that interests you the most.

Owning a niche bookstore allows a bookseller to explore their intellectual passion. Niche bookstores can help you to realize your personal passion because they are directed at a specific topic or audience. Bookstores that focus on a specific topic or specialty are considered niche bookstores. Children's, feminist, teacher, new age, mystery, science fiction, and political bookstores all are considered niche stores.

An excellent example of a very successful niche bookstore directed at the African American community is the Hue-Man Bookstore in Harlem, New York. The store is called "the hub for the Harlem community's longstanding and important tradition of African American letters." You can check out its website at **www.huemanbookstore.com**.

Is it For You?

If you have a great intellectual passion, or a hobby you are committed to, it might be an excellent source for your niche bookstore. But before you decide to create a niche store instead of a more general store, see if either of these two descriptions seems to fit you:

- I have an intellectual passion that I can consider myself an avid student of or an expert in. I have spent a number of years studying this subject. I have read many books on it, and I can converse readily about it. I may have worked in an industry related to this subject.

- I have a hobby that I love to read about, talk about, and hear about every day. I constantly am working at this hobby. I am involved with many other people who enjoy this hobby; I know where to get information about it, and how to connect to the community of others who enjoy this hobby, too. I would consider myself an expert at this hobby.

If you can honestly say that you find yourself in either description above, then a niche bookstore will be an excellent choice for you. Booksellers who have a bookstore devoted to a specific niche find their home away from home there, and their customers feel the same way.

Examples of Independent Bookstores

There are bookstores that feature every imaginable category or niche of book you can think of. Take a look below at the various types of bookstores owned by booksellers interviewed for this book — you will see a lot of diversity even in the small number of booksellers described here.

A Novel View

Location: Anchorage, Alaska

Pat Tegtmeier has created a used bookstore that allows customers to buy books, sell their own books, and even trade books. She has found a niche of happy readers in her market in which she is doing something different that appeals to her customer base. Her store also features a variety of interesting events that has made it a community meeting place. The store's website is **www.homestead.com/anovelview/index.html**.

Almark & Company Booksellers

Location: Toronto, Ontario

Al Navis, a rare book expert and dealer who has been in the old and rare book business for years, has built an interesting business that has definitely changed over time. With the advent of the Internet, much of Al's business has become by appointment only and over the Internet in an international market, causing him to move from his brick and mortar location to a large warehouse. He credits the Internet for completely changing the way he does business and making it much simpler, more far-reaching, and more successful. The bookstore's website is: **www. almarkco.com**.

Changing Hands Bookstore

Location: Tempe, Arizona

Gayle Shanks and her partners have combined the best of both worlds into an eclectic bookstore that sells both new and used books. Gayle and her partners have made events and book clubs a large part of what they do and have created a store that is a legend for readers in the Phoenix area. She and her partners have managed to bring celebrities and political figures to their store for appearances, including a recent book signing by Hillary Clinton. Changing Hands offers a number of interesting and related sidelines as well as a darling café, allowing book buyers to indulge their taste for the aesthetic, as well as their taste buds, simultaneously. The store's website is **www.changinghands.com.**

East End Books

Location: East Hampton, New York

John Brancati has amassed a wealth of book industry knowledge over 25 years as an executive for a major bookselling chain, Rizzoli's, and has created a high-end, exclusive bookstore of his own design. John has brought his business to the community he loves and has created a business that appeals to his exclusive and wealthy clientèle. John features guest appearances of well-known authors as well as a wonderful art gallery in his store. The store's website is **www.eastendbookstore. com**.

John K. King Used and Rare Books

Location: Detroit, Michigan

Owned by John King, this bookstore is a gigantic, multistory building full of used books. Employees working for John King actually keep in touch with one another through the use of walkie-talkies as they move throughout the giant store. King, who has been in the bookselling business since he was a teenager, loves to focus on used books and has made the used, old and rare book industry his business. The store's website is **www. rarebooklink.com**.

My Sisters' Words

Location: Syracuse, New York

Mary Ellen Kavanaugh created a place for those passionate about feminist literature to gather and form a community. After years of exposure to the world of retail through family businesses, she went whole-heartedly into a niche that fueled her passion for books and created a space for her customers.

She is proof that booksellers can use their stores to propel their ideas and intellectual passions. After sixteen successful years of creating that space for her readership, she decided to close her doors and explore other industry careers, but remains an expert in the feminist bookstore niche.

Take One! Film and Theater Books

Location: West Hollywood, California

Tim Morell has taken his years of theatrical book experience working for Samuel French, Inc. and opened his own store that caters to the show business community in West Hollywood, California. Tim has built a reputation for providing customers with industry expert seminars and workshops on topics that appeal to those in show business.

Tim has decided to expand his business and partner with a chain of acting schools, running his bookstore inside these schools in major cities in the U.S. He feels that this move will give him some national exposure in major U.S. cities as well as a strong marketing and Internet base for sales. Thinking out of the box, Tim has decided to move away from his traditional store and move forward with this interesting and nontraditional take on selling film and theater books in a way that lends itself to his perfect market.

That Bookstore in Blytheville

Location: Blytheville, Arkansas

Mary Gay Shipley has one of the only bookstores for miles in her small town. She has made it her business to listen to the needs of her customers and, over the years, has changed her business from one that mostly sold used books to military personnel stationed in the area to a bookstore that sells only new books and features a large children's section. She has perfected the art of listening and responding to the needs of her customers and built a thriving business at the same time. The store's website is **www.tbib.com**.

2.5 Developing Your Knowledge and Skills

Bookstore owners agree that finding out about what they need to do, and how others have done it in the past, greatly helps them avoid mistakes the first time they try something new.

You can keep developing your knowledge and skills using the methods described below. They include looking at how actual bookstores operate, and making connections with other people in the book industry who can help you learn. In chapter 7 of this guide you will also find some of the best resources including websites and industry publications.

2.5.1 Mystery Shopping

You have probably heard of mystery shopping, where companies hire people to go into their various retail outlets and pose as shoppers. This is an excellent way for management to get feedback about what their retailers are doing wrong — and right. In order to take a first-hand look at how other people are running their own independent bookstores, you can become your own personal mystery shopper.

Decide Where to Visit

To begin, take a look in your local Yellow Pages under "bookstores." If you live in the U.S., look at the American Booksellers Association's list of independent bookstores in your area. The Canadian Booksellers Association also allows you to search for bookstores near you. You might even want to visit some bookstores in your not-so-immediate area if they are especially related to the specialty or niche bookstore you are hoping to open.

- *American Booksellers Association — Bookstores in the USA*
  www.bookweb.org/bookstores/usa_states.html

- Canadian Booksellers Association — Find a Bookstore
  www.cbabook.org/find/default.asp

Making and Using Your Observations

Take time to visit several bookstores that interest you. As you go to a number of stores and record your observations, a couple of things will begin to happen. First, you will begin to know what bookstores are in your area and which, if any, will be competition for you. Second, you will get a chance to see bookstores in action. There is no substitute for seeing how bookstores really run and operate first hand.

Take a small notebook and pen so you can discreetly take notes. After you have been to each store, use the Bookstore Impressions Form on the CD-ROM to record your observations. On the next four pages you can see the form.

Bookstore Impressions Form

The Storefront

1. Is the store easy to spot from the street?   *Yes No*

2. Is it easy to park?   *Yes No*

3. Is there plenty of free parking or street parking?   *Yes No*

4. Is it an area with foot traffic?   *Yes No*

5. How is the area?

   _____

   _____

   _____

6. What kinds of people do you see on the street?

   _____

   _____

   _____

Entering the Store

1. What do you notice about the atmosphere?

   _____

   _____

   _____

2. What do you like about the way the store looks?

   _____

   _____

   _____

3. What do you notice about the physical layout of the store?

   _____

   _____

   _____

4. Does the store seem inviting or uninviting? Why?

   _____

   _____

   _____

5. Is the store clean?   *Yes   No*

6. Do you think you could get to a section you   *Yes   No*
   were looking for without assistance?

The Staff

1. Are you greeted?   *Yes   No*

2. Does the staff seem:

   Approachable?   *Yes   No*

   Pleasant?   *Yes   No*

   Bored?   *Yes   No*

   Crabby?   *Yes   No*

   Pushy?   *Yes   No*

3. When you ask a question, how do they respond?

   _____

   _____

   _____

4. Are they knowledgeable?   *Yes   No*

5. Are you able to get your questions answered to   *Yes   No*
   your satisfaction?

6. Does the staff make you feel comfortable   *Yes   No*
   about asking a question?

Using the Store

1. Can you browse easily?   *Yes   No*

2. Are you comfortable?   *Yes   No*

3. How is the lighting?

   _____

   _____

   _____

4. Are there places for you to sit?   *Yes   No*

5. How are the restrooms?

_____

_____

6. Are there any enjoyable extras, a café, etc.?   *Yes   No*

   What do they have?

_____

_____

7. Do you like the sidelines offered?   *Yes   No*

8. Do the sidelines fit the personality of the   *Yes   No*
   bookstore?

Merchandising

1. How are the book categories arranged?

_____

_____

2. What are the floor displays like?

_____

_____

3. Which books are shown face out?

_____

_____

4. What are the POP displays like?

_____

_____

Buying

1. Is the cash-wrap area organized?   *Yes   No*

2. Is it easy to get waited on?   *Yes   No*

3. Does the staff member speak pleasantly to you?   *Yes   No*

4. Do you buy?   *Yes   No*

5. What made you buy or stopped you from buying?

   _____

   _____

   _____

Leaving

1. What are your impressions when you leave?

   _____

   _____

   _____

2. Does a staff member notice you are leaving?   *Yes   No*

3. Does anyone thank you?   *Yes   No*

4. Does anyone say goodbye to you?   *Yes   No*

5. Do you feel positive about your experience?   *Yes   No*

Overall Impressions of the Store

1. What did you like the best about the store?

   _____

   _____

   _____

2. What did you like the least?

   _____

   _____

   _____

3. What did you notice about the store's logo, bags or other printed material?

   _____

   _____

   _____

4. Do you feel you will go back to the store in   *Yes   No*
   the future?

5. Will you recommend this store to anyone?   *Yes   No*

As you assess local bookstores, remember that what you see there should serve as ideas, not cast-in-stone certainties. There are no hard and fast rules about what your own store must carry.

In addition to observing booksellers anonymously, getting a bookseller's permission to let you observe them in action is also a wonderful way to learn. If you have a friend or a business contact that will let you spend a day seeing how they operate their business, it will be an excellent learning experience. If you don't know anyone who owns a bookstore, you can establish a contact and ask a bookseller for permission to observe.

See the next section for more information about how to approach a bookstore owner.

2.5.2 Contacting Bookstore Owners

If you can get a bookstore owner to talk to you, you can learn an amazing amount of insider information from someone who could be doing just what you want to do. Keep in mind, however, that while some may be quite willing to talk, others may be too busy. But if you ask nicely for information many people are very glad to share it.

> **TIP:** You will probably have a hard time if you approach a bookstore owner who could be considered your direct competition. There is a difference between sharing knowledge and giving away trade secrets. Make sure that the experts you try to contact are not your direct competition.

So, how do you contact bookstore owners? Just try the following steps:

- Identify what you are trying to accomplish by making contact

- Identify whom you think you should talk to

- Take the steps to make contact

For example, let's assume you went to a great bookstore in a neighboring town. First, find out the phone number and the owner's name. Then ask to speak to the owner.

Here is an example phone script:

> Hi, I am Betty Bookseller. I was in your store while I was on vacation and I really enjoyed it. Could you tell me who the owner is? *(After you are connected to the owner, John Infogiver, you proceed.)*
>
> Hi, John Infogiver? My name is Betty Bookseller and I am considering opening a bookstore in another part of the state. I was on vacation and had a chance to stop in your store, and I loved it.
>
> *(Now, ask permission to ask — an old sales trick.)* I was wondering if you would be willing to let me ask you a couple questions about how you do things? I could use some expert advice.
>
> **TIP:** It never hurts to tell experts you think they are experts. Usually they like being recognized for their accomplishments.

Make an appointment to call back the bookstore owner at their convenience. Then take some time and decide on a couple of questions you really want answers to. Ask only these questions. Also, offer to correspond in email if the expert prefers this.

Thank the expert for their time and make sure they know you appreciate the information. If you build this relationship slowly you can ask for more help and advice, and perhaps you can even find a mentor. Remember to:

- Ask permission to ask questions

- Be sensitive to the expert's time

- Decide ahead of time what you will ask

- Don't overwhelm your expert

- Build the relationship slowly and ask for more time at a later date

As you do research on the Internet, you will undoubtedly begin to see booksellers' websites that interest you. All of these sites have contact information you can use to directly ask for help and advice. Remember to adhere to the same advice in email that you use on the phone. Be courteous, brief, and grateful.

Below, you will find an example of a good email letter to request expert information. Use the example to help you decide what to write to an expert, but make sure that you make it original. Let your own personality and questions guide you in your letter.

Don't worry if you have to send out a number of letters before you have a response. Bookstore owners are busy people. If you are polite and persistent, many booksellers will be willing to talk to you.

Sample Information Request Letter

Dear John:

My name is Betty Bookseller. I am doing research online about bookselling because I am planning on opening my own used bookstore in Anytown, USA. I found your website at the American Booksellers Association website. I loved your website and admired the professional look and information on your site.

I am looking for an expert bookseller who wouldn't mind answering a couple of questions I have about the book industry. From the look of your site and what I can tell about your bookstore, I would be lucky to get a chance to speak with you.

If you would be willing to answer a couple of questions for me, I would truly appreciate it. I can call you, or if you prefer, I can correspond with you in email or whatever works for you. Please let me know if you would be willing to speak with me. Thank you in advance for your time.

Sincerely,

Betty Bookseller
Phone: (555) 555-1234
bettybookseller@email.com

2.5.3 Working in a Bookstore

There is no better way to learn than practical experience. This method – what some call "learning by doing" – is a way to really learn what goes on in a bookstore.

Apprenticing

Once you start contacting bookstore owners using the techniques described in section 2.5.2, you may discover opportunities to learn through apprenticing.

If you want to get real hands-on experience and pay back a bookstore owner for the opportunity to learn so much, you should offer to help a bookseller by working in their store for free. As an apprentice, you will learn the book business by doing. Experts and book professionals all agree that there is no substitute for hands-on training.

Getting a Job

Perhaps you want to have actual bookselling experience but you prefer, or need, to get paid for your time. Get a job in a bookstore! If you create time to work in a bookstore while you are planning your own venture, you will avoid many possible mistakes just by experiencing a variety of situations and how they are handled in a successful store.

Another bonus is that if you are an actual employee, you will be treated as an employee and not an apprentice or guest and you can learn a lot about how to deal with staff and employee policies and procedures, too.

2.5.4 Booksellers Associations

"We belong to the American Booksellers Association, Mountains and Plains Booksellers, Free Expression, Independent Booksellers Consortium, and probably more that I'm not thinking of right now. They give us a forum for sharing ideas, offer benefits like reduced fees for freight, insurance and charge cards, protect our First Amendment rights, and so on. We could not function without the support of these organizations."

— Gayle Shanks, Changing Hands Bookstore
Tempe, Arizona

National and regional trade associations give booksellers a chance to know one another and most see it as a way of connecting with people who share their personality traits, their passions, their experiences, and their commitments. Booksellers talk about book people as an unofficial club of people who are linked by what they do, their commitment to it, and the personality types that made them come to it in the first place. It is a close and congenial group.

A booksellers association is an excellent source for answers to almost any question regarding your new bookstore. Booksellers associations are designed to help booksellers form a strong collective and have a place to share information, educate themselves, and organize.

The American Booksellers Association

In the United States, the national booksellers association is called the American Booksellers Association, and it is located online at **www. bookweb.org**.

History

The American Booksellers Association was founded in 1900 as an association of booksellers across America who own retail bookstores. The ABA allows them to communicate nationally, share information and ideas, and promote their businesses.

General Information

You can join the ABA for an annual fee (starting at $350) that allows you a wide variety of benefits, including discounts with a number of important vendors, business management services, and on-going educational opportunities for both the new bookseller and the bookselling professional.

As a member, you will be eligible to join the BookSense program and link your bookstore's website to this online marketing tool. You will also have the ability to use the ABA website to access information and ask questions at the "Idea Exchange." The ABA produces an online magazine called *Bookselling This Week* that allows you to have up-to-the-minute information about industry news by simply clicking on the link.

The ABA is a vocal organization that speaks out on behalf of literacy, free speech and other important issues affecting the lives of booksellers and the readers who buy their books. The association presents an organized and strong lobbying voice in Washington.

Educational Opportunities For the Beginner

The ABA addresses the needs of people who are thinking about becoming booksellers and are looking for relevant information as they go through the process. A link on the ABA website allows you to access Open Learning Study Modules, including one by Barbara Theroux called "Introduction to the Book Business." The module provides a great deal of background information and then suggests a number of exercises to help you teach yourself what you need to know to get quickly up to speed.

BookSense — The ABA's Online Collective Presence

One of the major challenges that booksellers have in the Internet age is the availability of online book buying opportunities. The ABA has really created a wonderful solution to this that, in the words of one independent bookseller, "has saved the industry."

BookSense is a marketing tool that allows independent booksellers to have a collective Internet presence on the BookSense website (**www.booksense.com**), as well as have their own site on the BookSense network. You can read more about getting your own site in section 5.5.4.

American Booksellers Foundation for Free Expression (ABFFE)

Booksellers need to be concerned with free speech issues. The American Booksellers Foundation for Free Expression (ABFFE) was created in 1990 by the American Booksellers Association as "the bookseller's voice in the fight against censorship." ABFFE is concerned with protecting the right of individuals to exchange ideas, especially in books.

As a bookseller you need to be aware of how to protect the reading rights of your customers as well as your rights to obtain and sell the books you want to sell. You can visit the ABFFE's website at **www.abffe.org**.

ABACUS

ABACUS is another important tool that the ABA provides for member booksellers. Each year booksellers provide financial survey information so that the ABA can draw some important conclusions about how the independent bookselling industry is doing as a whole. This information is available to members. To find out more, visit **www.bookweb. org/education/abacus/5786.html**.

Trade Shows

The ABA's annual tradeshow, Book Expo America, is a vitally important book event. Booksellers from across the United States come together to interact, meet with publishers and others who sell to the book industry, and attend seminars, forums, and author sessions.

Booksellers attending the event can walk the trade show floor and see hundreds of publishers' booths, receive advanced reading copies of new books, and meet the individuals that they deal with face to face. Additionally, there is a full schedule of seminars covering important and current topics of interest for booksellers and other special events.

As an author I often attend the ABA because it gives me a chance to interact directly with publishers and booksellers, to view new books (including my own), talk to the people who I hope will both buy and sell my work, and to feel like I am at the pulse of the book industry. I have met a variety of people who have become colleagues and I have even sold book proposals. It is an amazing event full of energy and ideas, as all of the most important new books and the people who care about them are all together in one place at one time.

It isn't all work, and there are certainly some amazing events. I remember one evening event in which a number of well-known authors – including Amy Tan, Stephen King, and Dave Barry – all came together to form a rock band that performed as headliners at an evening event. I remember dancing to a tune sung by Stephen King and thinking to myself what a rare and unrepeatable experience it was to dance to a tune sung by one of the best-selling authors of all time. It was a remarkable evening and definitely an example of the up-beat attitude that surrounds this exceptional annual event. Visit **www.bookexpoamerica.com** for more information.

Trade Show Tips

Tradeshows are vital for the new bookseller. Where else can you come together with so many other booksellers at once and share so much? They are stimulating events designed to get attendees excited about what they do for a living.

No matter what tradeshows you attend as a bookseller, you have to know how to make the time you spend there work for you. How effectively you use the information you gather will determine the value of your investment. Consider the following tradeshow tips before paying attendance fees and booking hotel accommodations:

Why Are You Going?

Make sure you clarify for yourself why you are going. This is the first step in making your tradeshow time as effective as possible.

What do you hope to accomplish? Are you going to select publishers and wholesalers you hope to work with? Are you going to get a feel for what kind of books will be hot next season? Are you going to network with other booksellers? Are you hoping to attend a variety of panels and seminars and do some active learning about bookstore issues that concern you?

Have You Set Realistic Goals?

Do you have more than one goal? What do you think you can really accomplish? Remember, tradeshows are huge, exciting, and overwhelming. If you have a specific goal and you make plans to achieve it, then you will leave the experience satisfied.

Do You Have A Game Plan?

Most booksellers find that they are more successful if they make an organized plan and decide ahead of time what they will do each day. Focusing on one major goal per tradeshow and accomplishing it seems to work well for most people.

If you take a staff member along with you, coordinate your plans so you don't duplicate efforts. Working as a team means you can accomplish twice as much.

Are You Prepared?

Attending a tradeshow is a little like going to camp — you have to make sure you bring the things you need to have a good time.

Don't overdress or wear too many layers in what might be a hot room. One thing most tradeshow attendees swear by is a pair of comfortable shoes. Think about what you need for comfort, and bring it along!

Bring along a sturdy tote or other shoulder bag to carry materials you receive from booths on the tradeshow floor. While a lot of vendors give plastic bags to carry materials, they invariably break.

You should also carry a pen with you. As you receive cards from people at various booths, jot down a couple of notes on the card about your conversation or the contact person you met. At the end of the day it will be amazing how many cards you have. It's almost impossible to remember who you talked to.

Some tradeshow attendees carry a pocket tape recorder and make verbal notes about contacts and discussions as they walk a tradeshow floor. Others find it easier to communicate with their staff members if everyone brings a cell phone.

Talk to your reps ahead of time. If you are traveling to a show and hope to see a sales rep that you have an existing relationship with, contact them ahead of time to try to arrange a face-to-face meeting. It is great if you can actually connect with your reps in person at a show, but this is hard to do if you don't set it up ahead of time.

The Canadian Booksellers Association

The Canadian Booksellers Association (**www.cbabook.org**) is designed to provide the supportive collective for booksellers in Canada. According to a poll conducted by the CBA with its member bookstores, 83 percent of Canadian booksellers are optimistic about this season's sales. It's clear that most Canadian booksellers are feeling very positive about being in business and expect to be successful this year.

Services for Members

The CBA provides Canadian booksellers with a collective voice in Canadian government. The association similarly provides Canadian booksellers with many excellent benefits that assist them in their effort to succeed. Some of the highlights for booksellers include:

- Discounts for booksellers on credit and debit card processing

- A CBA member directory

- Freight discounts

- The Canadian Booksellers Magazine

- An annual trade show event — Book Expo Canada

Membership rates vary according to your gross annual sales volume. If you haven't opened your store yet, a provisional membership is available for around $130 for individuals who are planning to open their own stores. A student rate of around $25 is also available if you are a full-time university student.

Book Expo Canada

Book Expo Canada is a nationwide industry event for booksellers held annually in a major Canadian city. The conference features exhibitors representing all aspects of the book industry. In 2003, the trade show and conference attracted over 4,000 industry professionals, and of that number, more than 2,000 were booksellers.

Besides publishers, members can visit exhibitors of books on tape, inventory systems, fixtures and shelving companies, and companies who sell remainders. The event also features a variety of widely attended conference and seminar opportunities. See **www.bookexpo.ca** to find out more.

Regional Booksellers Associations

While there are definitely many important reasons to join a national organization, some booksellers also find it very beneficial to belong to a regional booksellers association. Booksellers report that regional associations give them the buzz on what is happening in their area. Regional associations allow you to network on a more personal level than you can on a national level.

Booksellers talk about how they really get to know members on a regional level and that the groups become a close-knit and helpful networking group. Additionally, it is less costly to attend a regional event because it takes place closer to home, which reduces travel expenses. Many booksellers like the intimacy of smaller shows.

Many regional booksellers associations produce their own holiday book catalogs that booksellers can use as part of their marketing campaigns. Also, many associations give annual regional book awards. See chapter 7 of this guide for a list of regional booksellers associations.

2.5.5 Educational Programs

"No matter what career people have been in, they need a little bit more information to get them positioned for their new careers as booksellers, to pick up the extra skills, to get the extra information, and especially to learn the idiosyncratic, quirky details of the book industry. "

— Donna Paz Kaufman, Consultant and Trainer
Paz & Associates, The Bookstore Training
& Consulting Group

For most new booksellers, opening a bookstore is an adventure. Like any new business experience, there are many things specific to the book industry that you will need to know to make your bookstore a success. Learning from others with proven track records as booksellers can be a wonderful way to see how it is done firsthand.

As mentioned in the previous section, booksellers associations offer a variety of workshops and educational programs at their annual conferences. Usually, these will focus on specific areas of bookselling. For a quick education in all aspects of owning a bookstore, consider one of the following programs:

Opening A Bookstore: The Business Essentials

Paz & Associates is a private consulting firm that helps new booksellers get started in the business. Their one-week program gives you a chance to discuss your plans and ideas with professionals who have business experience and can help you map out your personal plan for your bookstore.

They will look at your business plan, help connect you to resources in the industry, help you decide about your inventory of books, or just troubleshoot the specific problems you are encountering on your journey toward your store's opening day.

Class sizes are small (up to 20 people) and typically sell out up to a month in advance. The tuition is $1,200 for one person, and $990 for additional people from the same store. Paz & Associates also works with individuals as consultants for their specific needs.

Their website at **www.pazbookbiz.com** has information about their services and upcoming events.

Bookselling School

The Canadian Booksellers Association offers a two-day seminar called Bookselling School that teaches participants how to open and run their own bookstore. The program is run by Canadian booksellers with real world experience owning their own successful stores.

The program covers the important business aspects of opening your own bookstore, including:

- Finances

- Finding the proper location for your store

- How to negotiate a lease

- Inventory issues and decisions

- Advertising and marketing

The seminar also provides information about how to decide what type of bookstore you should open. Would-be booksellers attending the seminar report that what they learned gave them not only a plethora of information to begin, but the confidence to do so.

At the time of publication, Bookselling School cost $525 for CBA members or $625 for non-members. The 2004 session was held at the Metro Toronto Convention Centre in June during Book Expo Canada. For information about the next seminar visit **www.cbabook.org/school/default.asp**.

Choosing a Training Program

Consider these ideas when selecting a course or other fee-based learning opportunity:

- Be as clear as you can about what you need to learn. The better you can describe what you need, the better you can determine if the class or seminar will fit your needs and address your particular questions.

- Ask about the content of a course or seminar, or the process of a coaching session or consulting meeting. Find out what you can expect.

- Ask about price. Just like any other business issue, it is important to know up front how much any service you purchase will cost you.

- Ask about materials you will receive. Many bookselling seminars or classes include really helpful written information for you to take with you after it's over.

- Ask about follow-up meetings.

- Ask about reviewing your specific plans. Is there an opportunity for you to get help with your specific plans for your own store, or will the learning session be a general one? Both ways of learning are helpful, however, consultants will usually help you with your specific problems and questions while classes usually have a preset and less subjective curriculum.

3. Planning for Your Bookstore

At this point you may already know exactly what you want to do with your own bookstore. But if you are like most entrepreneurs, chances are there are many areas where you are still undecided.

This chapter can help you get greater clarity on what you want in your bookstore. It begins with a quiz to help you identify the type of bookstore that best suits your personality, then gives a variety of techniques to help you visualize your dream bookstore. Finally, it gives you practical planning tools to move from the idea stage to making your store a reality.

3.1 Identifying Your Ideal Bookstore Type

The following quiz will help you to determine what type of bookstore will best suit your skills, personal tastes, background, and personality. The quiz is a series of questions with multiple choice answers designed to help you hone in on the type of bookstore that fits your personality. While a simple quiz can't determine what is the only correct decision for you, it can help you clarify your strengths and those things that you may question, or need to learn, as you figure out what type of bookstore will be exactly the right one for you.

What Kind of Bookstore is Right For You?

Directions

As you answer the questions, keep track and add the score for each answer using the key at the end of the section. The results will help you to determine what kind of bookstore could be right for you.

1. **You buy some clothing for your sister's preteen child. The store you shop at is...**
   A. A funky resale boutique.
   B. Talbots.
   C. The Gap.

2. **On a free day you would rather go to...**
   A. A museum.
   B. A new art gallery.
   C. A flea market.

3. **You are on your way to buy a new chair for your home. You are probably looking for...**
   A. A rare antique dealer.
   B. A used furniture store.
   C. A department store's furniture department.

4. **You are deciding which restaurant to visit tonight. You may choose a...**
   A. Pricey fine gourmet restaurant.
   B. Trendy new deluxe eatery.
   C. Homey place you have been before.

5. **You are giving a friend a gift of flowers. You...**
   A. Go online and place your order with a national florist.
   B. Visit an expensive local florist known for her one-of-a-kind bouquets.
   C. Select a beautiful nosegay of flowers from your own garden.

6. **At Disneyland the attraction you prefer most among the following is...**

   A. Innoventions.

   B. The Disney Gallery.

   C. Great Moments with Mister Lincoln.

7. **You have an extra hour in a public library. You spend it...**

   A. Reading the *New York Times Book Review* online.

   B. Getting information from the friends of the library representative about a huge library book sale to be held over the weekend.

   C. Checking out *Old Books, Rare Friends: Two Literary Sleuths and Their Shared Passion*, by Leona Rostenberg and Madeline B. Stern.

8. **You have a chance to take a college extension course. The title of your course is...**

   A. "Recycled Art Experience."

   B. "King Tut's Treasures."

   C. "All About Your Wireless Camera Phone."

9. **You give your daughter a ring for her high school graduation.**

   A. It belonged to your grandmother.

   B. It came from a popular online jeweler.

   C. You bid for it successfully at an auction.

10. **You are traveling to a new city. You stay at...**

    A. A five-star hotel.

    B. A new place you read about in InStyle Magazine.

    C. A cozy bed and breakfast.

How to Interpret Your Score

First, use the answer key on the next page to determine the corresponding letter for each answer you chose. Next, count how many times you chose N, R, or U. Then, find out what kind of store could be right for you by seeing where your score fits below.

Answer Key

1.	A=U;	B=R;	C=N	**6.**	A=N; B=R; C=U
2.	A=R;	B=N;	C=U	**7.**	A=U; B=R; C=N
3.	A=R;	B=U;	C=N	**8.**	A=U; B=R; C=N
4.	A=R;	B=N;	C=U	**9.**	A=U; B=N; C=R
5.	A=N;	B=R;	C=U	**10.**	A=R; B=N; C=U

Mostly N's — New Book Store

You are a trendy person who loves what is new and coming on the scene. You are well informed, you are aware of technology, and you are up on current events. This attitude will help you own a new book store.

Mostly R's — Antiquarian Book Store

You love rare and classic things. You accept the best, you hunt for it, and when you find it you aren't afraid to pay for it. You love antiques, you are a collector, and you appreciate the best in everything. If this sounds like you, you may find yourself in an antiquarian bookstore.

Mostly U's — Used Book Store

You like homey, cozy things. You cherish things that are passed down from one person to the next, and you see the value in recycling and using things again. You are interested in the real lives of people from the past and may sometimes like things that are quirky, offbeat, or unique. A used book store might be a good choice for you.

Many N's and U's — Combination Book Store

You see the value in both new and used things. You aren't wasteful, and you value things that people can do and make themselves, but at the same time, you see the value in the new things the world has to offer. If you think this description suits you, a combination bookstore may be just what you are looking for.

3.2 Imagining Your Bookstore

In this part of the process, you will contemplate, explore, and imagine exactly what it is you are going to do with your bookstore. There are a number of tools and quick exercises that can help you through this process and guide your imagination into productive plans.

First you will learn how to daydream creatively and visualize your bookstore. You will then describe your ideas so you can use them to springboard your plans. Finally, you will create a series of pictures, or different ways of putting your ideas into form, so you can see them and touch them — and get excited about something real.

By becoming really clear about your idea, you will be able to move forward to the next step where ideas become action.

3.2.1 Visualizing Your Bookstore

Most people feel a little uncomfortable daydreaming — like they are doing something they aren't supposed to be doing. But in this case, daydreaming, or the ability to use your imagination to picture every detail of your bookstore, will help you move forward with your goal. Many experts call this technique "visualization," but you can think of it as creative daydreaming if you prefer.

Find a quiet place to sit and let your mind picture your "dream store." What would it look like? Where would it be? What do you see as you walk in the front door for the first time? Is it colorful? Is it fragrant? What kinds of people are browsing in the store? What is the lighting like? Is there a comfortable place to sit? Can you get a cup of coffee? Find a restroom? Try to see as many of the details as you can.

Here are some other questions to ask while imagining your bookstore:

- Where are you?

- What kind of store is it?

- How does it look from the outside as you walk up to the door?

- What do you see, smell, and hear as you approach your store?

- What sort of feeling do you have when you unlock the door and step inside?

- What colors and textures do you see inside?

- What is the mood of the store?

- Can you picture the layout of the store?

- What sort of books do you have?

- What special features do you notice?

- What do you love about the space?

- Is there anything truly unique about the setting that you imagine?

- What are the customers like?

- What is the staff like?

Try this exercise several times in several days and see how your visualization or daydream changes and evolves.

3.2.2 Describing Your Bookstore

Once you have created a satisfying daydream, it is time to write it down. Take a few moments and write a descriptive paragraph or two about your store as you have imagined it.

This written description can serve as a useful guide for you for many years. Put it somewhere where you can refer to it often — first, as you prepare to open your bookstore, and then later, as you move through the adventure of owning your own bookstore. Use it to reflect about where you are each step of the journey to measure how close to your ideal you have really come.

Refer back to the questions to ponder in the previous section to help you get started. You can even go through these questions one-by-one if you need to as you begin to write.

Try to use many vivid and colorful words to make your description as realistic and powerful as possible. Save your written description and look at it daily as you go through the process of creating ideas, researching plans, and setting goals for your new bookstore. As an example, I describe my dream store like this:

Sample Bookstore Description

As I approach my bookstore, I am happy to see how cute it looks from the outside. The old Victorian house has a garden full of flowers in front and a lovely wooden sign that spells out the name of my store in gilt letters.

As I walk inside, I see a small, cozy bookstore with lots of comfortable seating and stuffed, large chairs — big enough to curl up in and read. I see some old wooden tables and nice bright lights for reading that don't cause glare or eyestrain. I notice that there are some lovely potted plants adding a homey and natural air to the setting.

As I walk through the aisles I see a wide variety of new and used books, all attractively displayed. I see a really cute children's section with large stuffed animals sitting around on the shelves — with chairs and tables designed for children, but still comfortable enough for kids to share with their parents. I notice happy children and parents reading to their kids.

As I walk into another area in my bookstore, I see a room with chairs and tables and a slightly raised stage area, complete with lighting and a projection screen — a perfect space for guest authors and other experts to speak. I notice a seniors' book club meeting in which participants have moved the tables and chairs into an informal circle. Something funny must have just been read; I notice everyone is laughing.

I see a knowledgeable, happy staff waiting to help me, but not making me feel like I am rushed or under pressure to buy. I am aware of the peacefulness of the store. I notice that customers seem to be comfortable and reading, thinking, or sipping a cup of tea or coffee.

3.2.3 Creating a Picture of Your Bookstore

In order to move from an idea to a realized goal, it is necessary to see what you are aiming at. Pictures can help you to do this. You will need to see all aspects of the store you want to create. Expressing your ideas as something tangible is an important step before goal setting.

In this section you will learn how to do all of the following:

- Draw a simple bookstore sketch

- Create a "treasure map"

- Make a design board

- Experiment in a very simple way with the layout of your future store by making a very simple floor plan

By completing these simple tasks in the sections that follow, you will learn how to put your ideas into pictures and begin the process of making real your ultimate dream of owning your own bookstore.

Draw a Sketch

Take a moment to sketch your dream store. Sketching is a creative process that will help you think of details that may not have come to you as you visualized your dream store in the last section.

This exercise does not require that you have any artistic ability whatsoever. The idea behind making a sketch is that it is another way to access your creative imagination. Each method that you use to become clearer about your vision for your bookstore will help you to get closer to that goal!

TIP: If you are feeling motivated, you might want to make two sketches — an exterior and interior of what you feel your perfect store will look like.

Save this simple sketch as you go on to the next exercise, treasure mapping. You can transfer many of the ideas from your basic bookstore sketch to your treasure map.

Create a Treasure Map

Treasure mapping is a visualization or goal setting technique many people use to create a tangible picture of what they are trying to achieve. You don't need any artistic skill to make a treasure map. A treasure map is simply a tangible representation of a goal. Your treasure map should picture you achieving the dream of opening your own bookstore in as much detail as possible.

You can use any medium that works for you. Some people will draw or sketch, others will cut out pictures from magazines and make a collage, some will print off clip art from the Internet, and others will simply draw stick figures.

Follow these simple steps to make a treasure map:

- Get a piece of poster board — the type you might find in a super-market or stationery store that you would use to make a poster.

- Get pens, crayons, paint, glue, and magazines — anything that will help you picture your bookstore.

- Get a photograph of you to place in the treasure map to show you in your bookstore.

- Complete a picture that shows you in the bookstore of your dreams, happily existing and enjoying your success. You can label the picture, make little notes in different portions of it to describe what is happening, or do whatever you feel makes it a clear and powerful picture for you.

After you have completed your treasure map, hang it where you can see it every day. When you look at it, really try to see your bookstore in your mind's eye. If the picture changes in your mind, you can either add to your existing picture or make a new and updated treasure map.

Experts in the field of goal setting and creative visualization agree that making your goals tangible and real for you will help you to make them happen in reality.

Make a Design Board

A design board is a tool that interior decorators use to help their clients visualize the look and feel of a room.

Making a design board will help you to put together the colors and textures that you feel will make an impact in your store. When you actually have a store location and start thinking about paint colors, furnishings, fixtures, and window treatments, this exercise will help you make good decorating decisions.

The exercise is a simple one and can be added to over time. Just follow these steps to create a design board:

- Get a piece of poster board or another large piece of paper thick enough to be durable. Some people also use a bulletin board or cork board and pin or tack things on.

- Visit your local paint store and pick up a number of different paint sample cards. Glue or tack these on your board in the color combinations that you like the most and that you think would best convey the atmosphere you want for your store.

- Add fabrics, samples of tile and carpet, or anything else that you would like to add to your finished store. Usually you can get samples, or at least pictures of samples, from paint, tile, and carpeting stores.

Now when you actually have a store location and a place to paint, carpet, furnish, and decorate, you won't be starting from scratch. You will be able to use your design board to help you choose the colors, textures, and furnishings for your store. You will have time to decide what you love without making rushed or frantic decisions.

Experiment With a Floor Plan

A floor plan is a simple aerial view of your bookstore without any details. You don't have to be an architect to create a simple floor plan for your bookstore. In fact, you don't need any special tools — you can use a pencil and a piece of paper.

By playing around with the layout of your bookstore as you imagine it, you are creating a model to help you set up your actual store.

TIP: It's helpful to get a piece of grid paper, which will make sketching your layout easier.

Now sketch in the details of your floor plan. Use simple shapes and label them to denote various things in your layout. Think about where you want the doors, the windows, the bookshelves, the displays, the cash wrap area, and anything else you can think of.

Sample Floor Plan

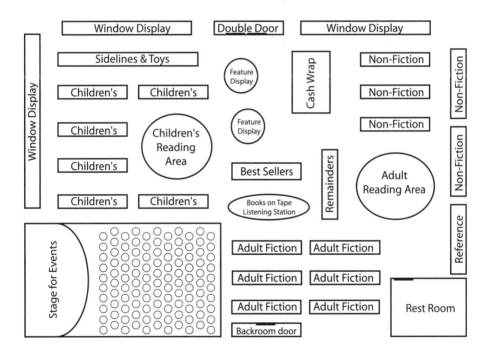

3.3 Setting Your Goal

By definition, a goal is your aim, your purpose, your target, or your aspiration. In this case, your goal is opening your own bookstore. Setting a goal allows you to organize all of your tasks into do-able, small pieces. To set a goal, it is always best to look at the major goal first, and then work backward until you know exactly what you need to do moment-by-moment to achieve the results you want.

The Major Goal

Naturally, your major goal is to open and sustain a bookstore of your own. Set your major goal using the description of your bookstore that you completed in the last section. For example:

> "My goal is to open a beautiful, trendy storefront bookstore selling new and used books for adults and children in the downtown Main street area of Somewhere, California, by one year from today's date."

How to Set Your Own Goal

Setting your goal is the first and most important step in attaining it. Look at the essential elements in goal setting below.

Understandable

A goal is a powerful statement that you can refer to again and again to help you stay focused on what you are trying to accomplish. As you write your goal, remember that it should be concise and easy to understand. It should summarize your plan in a sentence.

> **TIP:** Notice in the example goal above that the language is simple and concise — the sentence is short but it still contains all the important elements.

Exciting

A goal should make you excited. It should conjure up an image that makes you feel energized, happy, and positive about your plan every time you read it. Choose words that will help you stay motivated.

TIP: Use vivid adjectives to make your goal sentence exciting. Trendy, beautiful, funky, elegant — use words that help you to envision your goal.

Specific

To achieve a goal, you need to specify exactly what you want. Being specific is an important part of writing a powerful goal. The more precise and defined you make it, the more achievable it will be.

TIP: Describe and define your goal exactly. State what it is and where it will be. Use this portion of the sentence to stress pertinent information. Notice how the example says "storefront bookstore" and "downtown Main street area" and "books for adults and children" — each of these phrases are definite descriptions.

Scheduled

A goal must have a schedule. Your goal should state exactly when you will achieve it. By scheduling you make a commitment to complete tasks based on a calendar. Intentions are more easily realized when goals are definite.

TIP: Name a date. Notice how the example states "one year from today's date." It's even better to add the exact date to your goal.

Practical

Goals must be realistic — that is, they must be something that you can actually do. Look closely at your written goal and ask yourself if it is something that, given the proper time and resources, you will be able to do. Write your goal so that it is practical.

TIP: Notice how the example goal states a realistic amount of time to complete the goal, a location that isn't far-fetched, and a bookstore idea that sounds possible. In effect, the goal sounds like it can be done.

Now use the goal writing form on the next page to write your own goal. Post this goal where you can read it every day!

Goal Writing Form

Your name: _____

Today's date: _____

Goal Elements:

- Understandable
- Exciting
- Specific
- Scheduled
- Practical

TIP: Before beginning to write your goal, go back to the previous section and review the written description of your dream store as well as the other visualization experiences like your sketch, your treasure map, and your design board to get a vivid picture of your bookstore in your mind before proceeding.

My goal is...

_____

_____

_____

_____

_____

_____

_____

_____

_____

_____

_____

_____

3.4 Moving from a Goal to a Plan

Now that you have visualized your bookstore and made your ideas more concrete through writing about them and picturing them, you are ready to move from your goal to a plan that will help make your store a reality.

3.4.1 Brainstorming

Brainstorming is a technique used by businesspeople around the world to help them come up with ideas. By using this technique, you can start to develop a list of all the things you need to learn about, plan for, and do to make your new bookstore a success. Here are some basic rules to remember about brainstorming:

- Think of as many ideas, thoughts and questions as you can about opening your new bookstore.

- Don't judge yourself or stop yourself when you come up with ideas, thoughts, or questions. It's no fair telling yourself that an idea is silly, impractical, obvious, or anything else. The first rule of brainstorming is that all thoughts are good ones. Let yourself go!

- Write down ideas, thoughts and questions as they come to you. They don't have to be in any particular order.

- After you are done, use your brainstorm list to help you to make an action plan — a "to do" list of achievable tasks. You'll need a method to organize the information you come up with.

3.4.2 Using Checklists to Get Organized

An excellent way to organize the material you come up with during brainstorming is by developing checklists.

To get you started, this section includes six sample checklists consisting of sets of questions based on a typical combination bookstore. Many of the items in the checklists on the next few pages are things that most bookstore owners will need to think about and do.

The checklists have been divided by these important categories to help you quickly and easily move through the lists:

- Financial and Business Planning

- Physical Store

- Store Inventory

- Marketing and Advertising

- Technology

- Store Operations

These checklists are also included on the CD-ROM that comes with this guide. It is advisable to print the checklists so it's easy to add to them for your own reference.

As you read each sample checklist, think of the description of your own store. You will likely find that you need to add or subtract questions or develop additional checklists based on what you want for your own bookstore. In fact, you may want to keep the checklists nearby as you go through the rest of this guide so you can add items as you learn more about them.

Financial and Business Planning Checklist

1. What kind of bookstores are currently open in my area?
   _____
   _____
   _____

2. Has anyone successfully done what I am trying   *Yes No*
   to do before?

3. Are they still in business?   *Yes No*

4. Do I have any funding sources?   *Yes No*

5. How is my personal credit?
   _____
   _____
   _____

6. Can I get a loan?   *Yes No*

7. Where should I get a loan?
   _____
   _____
   _____

8. How do I get a loan?

_____

_____

_____

9. How much money will I need to start?

_____

_____

_____

10. How much money will I need to get an inventory of books?

_____

_____

_____

11. What should I include in my business plan?

_____

_____

_____

12. Will I use a business consultant to help me   *Yes No*
    write my business plan or other beginning
    financial documents?

13. Where will I do my business banking?

_____

_____

_____

14. Will I be a sole proprietor or will I form a partnership?

_____

_____

15. Will I incorporate my business?   *Yes No*

Physical Store Checklist

1. Will I open a new store or will I try to buy a store that already exists?

_____

_____

_____

2. Where will my store be located?

_____

_____

_____

3. How much square footage do I want?

_____

_____

_____

4. Will I lease a storefront or another type of store?   *Yes No*

5. What kind of fixtures will I get for my store?

_____

_____

_____

6. Where will I get them?

_____

_____

_____

7. How much rent can I afford?

_____

_____

_____

8. What kind of phone system will I install?

_____

_____

_____

9.   Will I need a computer cable modem installed?   *Yes No*

10. How will I lay out my store?

_____

_____

_____

11. What kind of furnishings will I have?

_____

_____

_____

12. What kind of lighting will I have?

_____

_____

_____

13. What will be on the walls?

_____

_____

_____

14. What will I do with the windows?

_____

_____

_____

15. What kind of decorations will I have?

_____

_____

_____

16. What is the overall "look" I am trying to achieve?

_____

_____

_____

17. What things do I own that I can use for my store?

_____

_____

_____

18. Will I need an installed alarm or will I hire a security service?

_____

_____

_____

19. If I have a café, what kinds of food will I serve and what vendors will supply these food items?

_____

_____

_____

20. Will I have special store bags or wrapping?   *Yes No*

21. Will I have a gift wrapping station?   *Yes No*

22. Will I have a unisex restroom or women's and men's restrooms?

_____

_____

_____

23. Will I need any construction or contracting work   *Yes No*
done inside my store?

What work will I need to have done?

_____

_____

_____

Inventory Checklist

1. Will I sell a variety of different kinds of books, or will I stick to a niche or specialty?

   _____

   _____

2. What categories will I sell?

   _____

   _____

3. Where will I get information about the books I should have?

   _____

   _____

4. How can I find out what new books are coming out?

   _____

   _____

5. What things are happening in national or world events that might impact my bookstore and the kinds of books I should carry?

   _____

   _____

6. How will I find books that relate to my niche or specialty?

   _____

   _____

7. What publishers will I buy from?

   _____

   _____

8. What wholesalers should I work with?

   _____

   _____

9.   Will I buy used books?   *Yes No*

10. Will I buy rare books?   *Yes No*

11. What sidelines should I sell?

_____

_____

12. Which vendors will I purchase sidelines from?

_____

_____

13. Will I buy remainders?   *Yes No*

14. Will I purchase books from customers?   *Yes No*

15. Will I sell music?   *Yes No*

What type of music will I sell?

_____

_____

16. Will I sell books on tape?   *Yes No*

17. What payment terms should I expect?

_____

_____

18. How will I organize my inventory?

_____

_____

19. What should I do with books that don't sell?

_____

_____

Marketing and Advertising Checklist

1. What will I do to advertise my bookstore?

   _____

   _____

   _____

2. Will I use newspaper advertising?   *Yes No*

3. Will I use radio or television advertising?   *Yes No*

4. Will I be listed in the yellow pages?   *Yes No*

5. Will I have a newsletter?   *Yes No*

6. Will I advertise through the mail?   *Yes No*

7. Will I advertise using email?   *Yes No*

8. Will I buy banner advertising on the Internet?   *Yes No*

9. Will I have a buyer's club?   *Yes No*

10. How will I get free advertising?

    _____

    _____

    _____

    _____

11. How do I write a press release?

    _____

    _____

    _____

    _____

12. Will I distribute flyers?   *Yes No*

    Where and how often?

    _____

    _____

    _____

    _____

13. What networking or business organizations should I join?

    _____

    _____

    _____

    _____

14. Who will create my logo?

    _____

    _____

    _____

    _____

15. Who will help design my sign?

    _____

    _____

    _____

    _____

16. How will I publicize events for my store?

    _____

    _____

    _____

    _____

Technology Checklist

1. What kind of computer system will I need?

   _____

   _____

   _____

2. What computer software do I need to get started?

   _____

   _____

   _____

3. What inventory, accounting, database or other software will I use?

   _____

   _____

   _____

4. Will I use software designed specifically   *Yes No*
   for the bookselling industry?

   What kind?

   _____

   _____

   _____

5. What security or firewall protection software will I use?

   _____

   _____

   _____

6. What Internet service will I subscribe to?

   _____

   _____

   _____

7. Is the space pre-wired for Internet?   *Yes No*

8. What kind of website will I have?

_____

_____

_____

9. Will I design the website myself?   *Yes No*

    What web design software will I use?

_____

_____

_____

10. How often will I update the website, and with what
    content?

_____

_____

_____

11. Will customers be able to purchase from my   *Yes No*
    store online?

12. Do I have enough computer knowledge to   *Yes No*
    set up my computer systems alone?

13. Who will I hire to help me with my computer systems?

_____

_____

_____

14. How will I back up my important computer files?

_____

_____

_____

15. Do I need any additional training to use my   *Yes No*
    store computers?

16. Will my staff?   *Yes No*

Store Operations Checklist

1. How much insurance will I need?

    _____

    _____

2. Will I hire employees?   *Yes No*

3. How do I find out laws about employees?

    _____

    _____

    _____

4. What about workers' compensation and liability insurance?

    _____

    _____

    _____

5. What about taxes? Sales tax?

    _____

    _____

    _____

6. Will I take credit cards?   *Yes No*

    How do I set that up?

    _____

    _____

7. Will I do my own books?   *Yes No*

8. Will I hire an accountant?   *Yes No*

9. Will I handle my own payroll?   *Yes No*

10. Will I do my own cleaning or hire a janitorial service?

_____

_____

_____

11. What are my legal responsibilities?

_____

_____

_____

_____

12. Who will be my attorney?

_____

_____

_____

13. Where do I get a business license?

_____

_____

_____

14. What kinds of forms will I need to complete for the city, county, state, and federal government?

_____

_____

_____

_____

15. Will I play music in my store?   _Yes No_

How do I go about paying music licensing fees?

_____

_____

_____

16. Will I join booksellers associations?　　　　*Yes No*

　　Which ones?

　　_____

　　_____

　　_____

　　_____

17. What trade or professional journals and magazines will I
　　need to subscribe to?

　　_____

　　_____

　　_____

18. Which trade shows and conferences will I attend?

　　_____

　　_____

　　_____

19. What kind of outside consulting help might I need?

　　_____

　　_____

　　_____

20. What seminars or educational courses should I attend?

　　_____

　　_____

　　_____

3.4.3 Creating an Action Plan

Now that you have identified questions you need to answer and items to
look into, you are ready to determine the various milestones that you will
need to achieve your major goal. In this section you will choose your
milestones and break them down into organized tasks.

What is an Action Plan?

An action plan is exactly what it sounds like — your plan of action. For each task you want to accomplish you will need to complete a series of smaller tasks to accomplish the larger one.

An action plan is really a glorified "To Do" list. If you have ever made a to-do list for yourself, you already have the basic skills to make an action plan. Here are the things you will do when you make an action plan:

- Describe each task

- Estimate how long each task will take

- Estimate the cost for each task

- Designate a person/s to complete the task

- Decide on a completion date for each task

It's important to be clear about the terminology of action planning so it doesn't get confusing. In this book we use the following action planning terms:

- **Milestones:** The really big things you need to accomplish to achieve your goal

- **Tasks:** The important things you will do to accomplish each milestone

- **Subtasks:** The more trivial things you will have to do to complete a task

For example, setting up your physical store is a milestone. The things listed on your brainstorming checklist to accomplish are tasks, and what you will have to do to complete each task are subtasks.

Deciding on Action Steps

An action plan is all about the action. For each task you previously listed on your checklists, you will need to brainstorm the steps to take to complete the task. Sometimes you will realize that there are a couple of complete tasks you need to do before you can move to something else, and other times you will realize that completing a task will be a one-step process.

Often you can cluster tasks, meaning you can get several done at the same time. It makes sense for you to cluster some of the tasks that naturally need to be done together. For example, you may want to have a consistent design throughout your whole store. It makes sense, then, to pick out the couches and the chairs to go with the tables, the wallpaper and paint for the store to match your overall color scheme, and so on. Clustering tasks saves time.

> **TIP:** As you set your goal and determine the milestones and tasks necessary to open your bookstore, it's important to remember that it is a work in progress. Your plan will alter as you gather more information and complete various tasks. Since all bookstores are different, the milestones and the tasks you choose to complete will be unique to your store. Expect to change and refine your plan as you go along.

Making a clear and organized plan before you begin will save you lots of time and money! Take a look at the sample task worksheets on the next two pages to see an example of an organized task.

Sample Action Plan Task Worksheet #1

Task Description:

_____

_____

_____

Person/s to Complete Task:

_____

_____

Subtasks:

1. _____

2. _____

3. _____

4. _____

5. _____

6. _____

Estimated Time to Complete:

_____

_____

_____

Estimated Cost:

_____

Expected Completion Date:

_____

Notes:

_____

_____

_____

Sample Action Plan Task Worksheet #2

Task Description:

Install Internet cable modem throughout store. Each room in the store should have cable installation so computers can access the Internet. Additional modem jacks should be available in community room for guest speakers and customer users.

Person/s to Complete Task:

Me, maybe Bob, and hired vendor.

Subtasks:

- Research available cable modem providers.
- Talk with new landlord about existing cable modem jacks and his part in making sure building is Internet ready.
- Find out what other hardware is necessary. Will I need more high-speed modems?
- Call vendor and discuss options and cost.
- Decide on which vendors will provide services and settle on installation and monthly costs.
- Schedule installation.
- Learn how to connect cable modems, upload software, boot and reboot and teach staff.

Estimated Time to Complete:

Three weeks. One week for research step, one week to finalize deal and schedule installation, and one week to make sure everyone is trained on the new procedures.

Estimated Cost:

No idea. Add this later after initial research.

Expected Completion Date: June 5, 2006

Moving Forward with Your Action Plan

Now that you know the basics of action planning, here are the steps to move forward with your own action plan:

- Organize the brainstorm checklists in the order you would like to complete them. When doing this, think about what milestone category you think you will need to begin first, second, and so on. For example, you need financing before you can get a physical location. You probably want to set up your technical systems before you get your inventory. Take some time and determine in what order you will complete the milestones.

- Complete an Action Plan Task Worksheet for each task you determine in each milestone category.

- Get a binder. Organize the milestones as category dividers and insert all of your completed task worksheets in each category.

Software to Assist with Planning

For some people, printing off hard copy lists and organizing them in a binder will be frustrating. If you are computer-savvy, consider organizing your action plan with good project management software like Microsoft Project, Project Kickstart, or Fasttrack Schedule.

- *Microsoft Project*
  www.microsoft.com/office/project/prodinfo/default.mspx

- *Project Kickstart*
  www.projectkickstart.com

- *Fasttrack Schedule*
  www.aecsoft.com

You can also use software to develop a Gantt chart. Gantt charts look like a glorified bar graph but they are better than traditional timelines because they allow you to see and compare the length of specific tasks as they compare to other tasks. You can see examples at **www. smartdraw.com/resources/centers/gantt/index.htm,** which is the website for SmartDraw, a software program that can create Gantt charts.

3.5 Creating a Business Plan

A business plan is an organized, well-researched, brief look at every aspect of your business. While your action plan is filled with specific steps for you to follow, your business plan is designed to give other people an overview of your business. Business plans are typically created so that someone trying to open a business can approach lenders or investors for financing. Because of this, it is very important that your business plan makes the reader feel confident that your business will succeed.

Creating a business plan can be valuable to you for reasons in addition to financing. A good business plan outlines your business clearly, and makes you take a look at many things that you might forget or not focus on if you didn't go through the process of creating one. This section will show you how to write a good business plan. You may also find additional resources online at the websites below:

- *Small Business Administration: Writing the Plan*
  www.sba.gov/starting_business/planning/writingplan.html

- *Creating an Effective Business Plan*
  http://home3.americanexpress.com/smallbusiness/Tool/biz_plan

You may also wish to purchase a software program that will help you create a business plan. An example of such software is Business Plan Pro 2005, which is available for $99.95 at **www.paloalto.com/ps/bp.**

Some business owners seek help from consultants when writing a business plan, especially in the areas of market research and financial projections, which can be challenging. Consultants are admittedly expensive, but can offer skills and expertise that will save you money once your business is operating. Before looking for a consultant, review your start-up budget to be sure you have room for the expense.

A good business plan includes:

- A table of contents

- An executive summary

- A description of your business

- A market analysis and marketing plan

- Financial statements

- An operations plan

- Management and staffing plan

- Appendices

3.5.1 Table of Contents

A table of contents will let your potential lenders move through your business plan with ease. The best way to make the table of contents is to write the rest of your business plan first, and then complete this step last.

3.5.2 Executive Summary

An executive summary is a one or two page summary of what you are trying to do. They are called executive summaries because they are concise – but comprehensive – looks at the most pertinent parts of a plan — similar to the type of report a busy executive might prefer. While your full executive summary will be a bit longer, here is a sample of what you are aiming for in this part of your business plan:

Sample Executive Summary

Readersville Bookshop will serve the western downtown business district and adjacent residential area. Customers will be from law offices, major hotels, bed and breakfasts, nearby apartments, condominiums, and middle-income family households. The Bookshop will use 1,200 square feet of an historical building, located between a cafè and hair salon. A five-year lease will cost $1,500 per month plus utilities. Start-up costs of $32,000 will come from the owner's personal investment. The owner and manager have retail bookstore experience, business management training, and college educations in literature and English.

3.5.3 Description of Your Business

The description of your business is important — it has to get the attention of potential lenders. Lenders must be convinced that your business idea is well thought out, thoroughly researched, and practical. Lenders need to be able to picture your business clearly.

You will describe the following in this section:

- **Your products and services.** These may include books, stationery, newspapers, magazines, note cards, greeting cards, readings, kids' story time, special book orders, and gift certificates.

- **Customers.** Are you selling to businesses or individuals? What are your target market's typical occupations? Are you selling to families? Retirees? How will you market to them? This topic will be covered in more detail in your section on market analysis, but for now give an overview, as in the sample that follows.

- **Goals.** What will you accomplish by establishing your bookstore?

- **Store appearance.** Describe the location, windows, signage, square footage, merchandise displays, and traffic flow into and out of the store.

- **Unique features.** Why is your bookstore needed? What will it contribute to the community? What are its strengths over competitors? This will also be part of your marketing section.

- **Management.** Cover the store's ownership and legal structure, number of employees, and their background, experience, and relevant education.

- **Start-up.** An overview of financing amounts, sources, business registration, and insurance. This will be a summary, and details will follow in your financial section.

Note that your business description is meant to give an overview of the features listed above. Some parts of your business description may overlap with information you provide in detail on marketing, finances, operations, and staff as you compose the rest of your business plan. A sample business description is included on the next few pages.

Sample Business Description

Products and Services

Readersville Bookshop plans to sell primarily used books, 60 percent of which will be paperback and 40 percent hardcover and collectibles. The books will be both fiction and nonfiction, in categories that include mass paperback best-sellers, mystery, romance, western, science fiction, literature, crafts, cooking, home improvement, art, music, biography, history, politics, military, psychology and social sciences, business and careers, law, health and healing, spirituality, women's studies, and sexuality. Both adult and children's books will be sold, along with books on parenting and education.

Sidelines in the store will include audio books, newspapers, greeting cards, note cards, book covers, bookmarks, and original art of community artists.

The Bookshop plans to participate in several special community events, including monthly art receptions and exhibits for local artists, a business block party in the summer, an annual book discussion in conjunction with the "community reads the same book" event, and occasional free musical performances.

Bookshop staff will perform special book searches and orders for customers. Gift certificates will be available. Modifications to inventory will be made according to customers' interests.

Customers

The Bookshop's target market includes business workers at shops, hotels, law offices, and a new state courthouse constructed last year that is only two blocks away. Tourists will be drawn from three major hotels within six blocks and five bed-and-breakfast accommodations within two blocks of the Bookshop.

Approximately 30,000 households reside within walking distance, and census data estimates put the median household income in the area at $46,500. The median age is 35, with 10 percent of the population under 5 years of age and 13 percent between 45 and 54. Population growth for the next five years is projected at a healthy 7 percent.

Marketing strategies will be directed toward identifying the interests and needs of these potential customers by distributing promotional brochures to businesses and residences, and by conducting surveys in the bookstore and polls on the Bookshop's website.

Goals

The primary goal of the Bookshop is to provide a unique blend and variety of affordable books and services to both community residents and visitors, in a small-business setting that will charm the hearts and satisfy the minds of customers, with a long-term goal of becoming a community gathering place and discussion salon.

The vision of success for the Bookshop is based upon five values:

- Satisfied customers
- Good reputation
- Ability to pay fair wages and offer training opportunities to staff
- Ethical business behavior
- Quality products and services

Store Appearance

Readersville Bookshop will be located in the western edge of the downtown business district in a free-standing, historical two-story building built in 1920. The Bookshop will be on a busy one-way street between a popular cafe and a trendy hair salon and spa, and directly across the street from a fine dining establishment and various business offices.

The building is accessible by public sidewalk, and both sides of the street have metered parking. One free parking spot adjacent to the building will be available to customers. The public bus stop is one block away.

A sandwich-board sign will sit at the corner, half a block away, pointing to the store. A window mural with the store's name will be painted on one side of the porch facing oncoming traffic, and a sign with the store's name will hang from the front of the porch roof.

Inside, approximately 1,080 square feet of space will be used for books, organized on bookshelves and their categories identified by small wooden signs. The main floor will hold the most popular types of paperback fiction, and signs will direct the browsing customer upstairs for nonfiction and down to the basement for the science fiction sections. Upstairs, there will be two rooms divided by a narrow pass-through where collectibles will be displayed. One of the two rooms will be devoted to children's books, along with books on parenting, education, and pets.

A number of windows permit light on all four sides of the building. Both rooms upstairs have large windows at each end, allowing penetration of both morning sun and evening sunset. The basement has no windows, enabling 7-foot bookshelves to surround the room and utilize the space fully.

On all three levels, books will be displayed on tables and tops of bookshelves, along with live indoor plants. Some posters will be displayed on the walls, except when the space is needed for shows of local artwork.

Initially, the store will be open seven days a week during the spring and summer, and will be closed on Sundays during the fall and winter months.

Unique Features

Among the Bookshop's unique features is a grassy side yard with a fine old birch tree that will grace the book fairs and other promotional activities to be held there during the spring and summer months. Flower boxes line the sidewalk leading up to the entrance, which is an enchanting covered porch with hanging flower boxes. Red and white geraniums with blue trailing lobelia in the flower boxes will add charm and invite customers inside.

Weary shoppers will be able to sit on a picnic bench on the porch, and at the proper time of day watch the sunset go down in the west. Being an historical building will make the Bookshop one-of-a-kind and offer a comforting alternative to large, square bookstores with fluorescent lights.

The July 2002 *Inc.* magazine featured an article on "America's Favorite Hometown Businesses," described by well-known writers, entertainers, and influential people. Not surprisingly, they included such places as a comic bookstore in New Jersey, a bookstore with a literary salon in New Orleans, and an old-fashioned bookstore café in Maryland owned by the husband of popular novelist Nora Roberts. The theme for the issue was "Everything Small is Big Again," which identified trends toward quality and comfort in both home life and the business world. These are the unique features that the Bookshop will bring to the community.

Management

The Bookshop is licensed to begin operations as an independent bookstore, woman-owned sole proprietorship. The sole proprietor will assume full responsibility for all financial management and major administrative functions.

A family member will be hired on salary at $25,000 per year as the full-time manager. A part-time employee will be hired at minimum wage or more, depending on experience, and trained to assist in sales and stocking during busy times, particularly during the summer tourist season. Both owner and manager have retail bookstore experience with education in English and business management.

Start-Up

On start-up, the sole proprietor will purchase the inventory of an existing bookstore that is closing after ten years standing in the community. Start-up costs for inventory are $32,000 and include all books and store fixtures, plus two weeks of training by the seller.

Additional start-up costs include $1,300 for a new computer/printer package, deposits on utilities and rent, business license, annual liability and workers' compensation insurance, attorney fee for review of lease, accountant's fee for review of seller's financial statements, supplies, signage, brochures, business cards, and a membership fee to the regional booksellers association.

All start-up costs and full operating costs for the first six months will be paid using the owner's personal funds.

3.5.4 Market Analysis

A market analysis tells potential lenders precisely why your business will succeed in today's bookstore market, based on what the market has to offer.

Take the time to get out into the world to see what other bookstores are there. Think about how you will position your bookstore in the marketplace, and who your competition and customers will be, then put the details into your market analysis.

Your Product

Naturally, your main product will be books. But it is helpful to define exactly what kind of books you will sell. If you run a theatrical bookstore, your book inventory will be far different than if you run a store specializing in New Age literature.

But there is more to your product than just your inventory of books in your bookstore. Think about the total experience you are selling. Perhaps you will sell food at your bookstore's café, or perhaps your sidelines are an important part of what you will sell. Will you have events or seminars that you charge for? To determine your product, you need to include everything you are going to sell.

Your Customers

Even before you open your doors for the first time, you can decide who you believe your customers are, and over time you will get a chance to see how this idea grows and possibly changes. Your customer base will develop based on the kind of bookstore you have, or your bookstore's niche in the marketplace.

If you choose an upscale store in a resort town, your customers will be working professionals and tourists who are leisurely shopping or sightseeing. If your store is right across the street from your local university, you are probably going to cater to students and academics. You have a lot of control over the kind of customers you attract by the niche in the market your bookstore fills.

Once you have thought about who it is you are trying to attract to your bookstore, you can target your market. Targeting your market means going after the segment of the market that you feel will be your best customers. The best way to do this is to define a segment at a time.

For example, some easy-to-define market segments for a bookstore across the street from a university might include professors, new students, researchers, and the children of professors and students. These are all distinct segments of your target market and defining them will help you figure out:

- What sort of ads to place.

- What magazines, newspapers, and other print media to use for your ads.

- What other media you might use for advertising.

- What sort of events to have inside and outside your store.

- What kinds of promotions will attract each specific segment of your target market.

For example, in order to attract professors to your store, you will run a different ad in a different media source than you would use to attract new students.

The key to being able to target your market effectively is to figure out as much as you can about the segment you are trying to attract. You need to figure out what they read, where they eat, where they live, where they hang out, what radio stations they listen to, and so on. Once you do, you will know how to reach them.

Your Competition

Another important aspect of defining how to pursue your market is to figure out who your competition is. In the case of a college town bookstore, you might be in competition with an on-campus bookstore, a competing neighborhood bookstore, a superstore, or an Internet bookstore that your population will use because doing so is easy for them.

Observe your competition. What are they doing to advertise? What sort of events do they have? Who do their customers seem to be? Visit other bookstores and note what attracts your eye and what you like or dislike about what you see. Your plan can address areas where your competition falls short, or mimic things that you admire.

Finding out about your competition helps you hone in on your own uniqueness — what you can do differently, and, in the case of a true competitive spirit, better. Also, being clear about your competition's target market will help you make key decisions about the customers you want to pursue and how you want to pursue them.

Market Information Resources

Some resources for your market analysis may include:

- Your local chamber of commerce.

- Your local or state Convention and Visitors Bureau.

- Your local bank, which can provide information on economic trends and forecasts.

- Your daily newspaper, particularly the business section, which will have details on community business trends and new competitors.

- Your state's Department of Labor, which uses census and other data to prepare reports for community use.

- The U.S. Census, which breaks down into community census tracts and zip code areas. Especially relevant is the economic census for bookstores, conducted every five years, most recently in 2002. You can view this report online at www.census.gov (click on the link for "economic census," then the Industry Series List and Schedule to find bookstores in the "retail trade" section).

- Other booksellers' advertising materials, which may provide information that can help you stay competitive. If a competitor is advertising that it has the community's largest book inventory with 500,000 books, you can use this to your advantage by emphasizing your store's unique features — its "great selection of books in hometown comfort," for instance.

- Advertising offices of local media and private media marketing agencies. Look up "Market Research and Analysis" in the Yellow Pages.

- Trade associations, such as your regional booksellers association, the American Booksellers Association, Antiquarian Booksellers Association, Publishers Weekly, and publishers' representatives who serve your area. See section 7.1 for links to bookseller association websites.

A sample market analysis is included on the next page.

Sample Market Analysis

The Readersville Bookshop will serve the western downtown business district and adjacent residential area. Customers will be drawn from law offices, bed and breakfasts, and major hotels, and from nearby apartments, condominiums, and middle-income family homes. Approximately 30,000 households reside within walking distance.

Census data estimates put the median household income in the area at $46,500. The median age is 35, with 10 percent of the population under 5 years of age and 13 percent between 45 and 54. Population growth for the next five years is projected to be a healthy 7 percent.

The nearest competitor in the downtown area is 10 blocks away and specializes in new books and gift sidelines. Other bookstores in the community, including large national retailers, are located in suburban malls.

Demand for used books in general appears to be growing, with the used-book store business itself showing an upsurge in popularity and profitability. An article in the August 11, 2003, issue of *Newsweek* ("Secondhand Prose" by Malcolm Jones) tells us that the used-book market, consisting mostly of small, independent retailers, has grown more than 20 percent since 1992, and that "Used-book stores now occupy the hot corner of the bookselling trade."

Our knowledge of the market will grow once the Bookshop is operating and we have the chance to observe and get to know our patrons. We will also conduct in-store surveys to gain feedback about customer needs and interests. As recommended by the Small Business Administration, the Bookshop intends to remain flexible with respect to the market and continually reassess, readjust, and refocus as conditions change.

3.5.5 Marketing Plan

Just like all the other aspects of your preplanning, you will need to spend some time figuring out who you think your customers will be and what you can do to get them to come through your door.

You can use your detailed knowledge of your target market and competition to devise a personalized marketing plan (also known as a *market strategy*) for attracting customers to your bookstore. Choose specific marketing techniques suitable for your particular situation.

Here are some tactics you might include in your market strategy:

- **Advertising.** Will you market your store through the Yellow Pages, media, door-to-door flyers, brochures, or complimentary bookmarks? Who will receive or distribute your ad materials? How much or what percentage of your budget do you plan to spend on each type of ad?

- **Publicity.** You might promote special activities and events by submitting announcements to the media as press releases.

- **Website.** Will you create and maintain a web presence and consider selling online? Will you let customers sign up for a regular e-mail newsletter describing new releases, upcoming events, and store promotions?

- **Name recognition.** You can promote name recognition by using your logo in advertising, brochures, bookmarks, stationery, signs, and on your website.

- **Training.** Will you attend bookseller tradeshows, marketing workshops run by the Small Business Administration, and other events?

- **Community goodwill.** You can form a partnership with a school, contribute merchandise or gift certificates for non-profit fundraisers, donate excess books for literacy, or offer discounts to teachers or loyal customers. If you plan to maintain friendly business relationships with your competitors, they may refer a customer your way when they can't fill his or her needs.

- **Special events.** You can schedule book club meetings, lectures, art exhibits, and author appearances.

Sample Marketing Plan

Prior to opening Readersville Bookshop, the owner and manager will attend the regional booksellers association tradeshow and complete the training workshop on opening a new bookstore. The tradeshow will be an orientation to the local world of book publishers, publishers' representatives, distributors, and wholesaler discounts. Our start-up budget includes the $1,500 in expenses associated with the tradeshow and training.

We will also use start-up funds to cover the one-time cost of purchasing and installing the front porch signage and the sandwich-board sign that will be placed on the corner a half block from the store. The cost for this one-time signage will be $500.

Five percent of the Bookshop's budget will be allocated for advertising and marketing expenses, including $1,000 for a "Grand Opening" media blitz on radio stations and in daily newspaper display ads. Our advertising will focus on presenting the Bookshop as a neighborhood bookstore for residents and businesses, and as a friendly and convenient shopping spot for visitors.

Marketing within the first few months of operation will include hand-delivered brochures and personal contact with nearby businesses, a strategy that market analysis suggests will be effective.

We will distribute approximately 10 introductory brochures to each of the three major hotels and five bed and breakfast establishments in the area. We will distribute another 200 to the local Convention and Visitors Bureau to display in the visitors center. Flyers will be distributed by the local paper to approximately 30,000 households in the census tract area for a cost of $0.02 each. The printed material will include features about the children's book room and upcoming storytelling sessions.

Total Marketing Budget: $3,500
* based on 5% of $70,000 operating budget

Marketing Budget Breakdown

Media blitz	$ 1,000
Brochures at start-up (600)	60
Brochures (300 monthly for 11 months)	330
Business cards and stationery	110

Bookmarks (2500)	$ 375
Flyers (30,000)	600
Yellow Pages ad	360
Discretionary advertising	665

Additional market strategies will include in-store surveys designed to identify the interests and needs of potential customers. A website has already been created and will be maintained at no cost by a friend; the website content will include book reviews, notices of special events, and a poll to collect additional information on customer needs.

3.5.6 Financial Plan and Statements

Here you need to tell potential lenders how much you think it will cost to operate your bookstore, what you expect your sales to be, and what profit margin you expect. Lenders will want to see if your bookstore is a good risk for their money. This is where you prove to them that it is.

Lenders want to know exactly how you will spend the money they give you. This portion of the plan must give lenders real numbers to crunch. According to the American Booksellers Association's Manual on Bookselling: Practical Advice for the Bookstore Professional:

> "In addition to the basic costs of construction, fixtures, and inventory, there will be costs for in-store equipment such as telephones, a fax machine, computers, cash registers, and calculators. There are the costs of dues and subscriptions for professional organizations and publications; deposits and fees for utilities, consultants, attorneys, and accountants; and a security deposit as part of your lease agreement (often three months' rent). In addition, you need to set aside money for advertising and promotion (including an ad in the Yellow Pages), as well as for supplies such as bags, wrapping paper, order forms, and gift certificates."

Further excerpts from the manual can be found at **www.bookweb.org/join/1456.html**. You can get an idea of what other booksellers spend by reviewing the industry averages published by the American Booksellers Association in its annual ABACUS study. Go to **www.bookweb.org/education/abacus** to view the 2003 results.

In an article published in the August 16, 2002, *Business Journal of Jacksonville*, author and book industry professional Donna Paz Kaufman said that independent bookstore owners can expect to make, at best, a gross margin of 40 percent and an average net margin of 1.5 to 5 percent.

As this topic is a complex one, we have covered it in detail later in this guide. See section 4.3 for detailed advice on and samples of how much to budget for your initial inventory of books and information about the other items you will need to start your business.

3.5.7 Operations Plan

The simplified way of looking at this part of the business plan is to describe what you are planning to do and how you are planning to do it. Describe your store — where it is, what it looks like, and its features. Discuss what books you are going to sell and where you will get them, and take lenders through the steps required to operate your bookstore.

Your operations plan should be detailed, and build on the information provided in the business description section of your business plan. It should cover the following:

- **Store Location and Premises.** Will you be renting, purchasing, or building your bookstore? Where is your store located, and who are your neighbors? What is the neighborhood like? Where will customers park? Is there public transportation nearby? How large is your store, and what are its features, inside and out? How will you organize your selling space? Will your store include a café? Will you provide comfortable chairs for customers who want to sit and read? Will you play music?

- **Inventory.** What categories of books will you sell, and will they be new or used? What types of sidelines will you sell? What will your starting inventory contain? If you're selling used books, how will you build your inventory? How often will you purchase new inventory? Where will you store new inventory, and how will you move it to the floor? How will you display featured books and sidelines? What will you do with damaged or unsold inventory? Will you have a return policy? How will you keep track of inventory?

- **Hours of Operation.** What days and hours will your store be open? Will you have special holiday and weekend hours?

- **Suppliers.** Who will you purchase your books from? How will suppliers ship your books? What are your suppliers' return policies? Where will you find out-of-print or rare books? How will you compensate customers who provide used books? Where will you acquire sidelines and, if you're opening a café, food and beverages and restaurant supplies?

- **Equipment.** What type of computer and software will you use? Will you have a printer, scanner, fax machine, or photocopier? How many phones will you need? What type of cash register will you use? How will you process debit and credit card payments? Will you use a dolly or other equipment to move inventory? What equipment will your café need? Will you install a security alarm? What kind of shelving will you use?

- **Plans for Growth.** Do you have a strategy for growing your business? Do you plan to expand your inventory? Will you add new book categories or sidelines? Will you move to a larger location? Do you plan to open a second store? What financial risks do you face in opening your bookstore? Do you have a plan for minimizing these risks?

While your operations plan will be more complex and specific to your business, here is a sample of the tone and type of information to provide:

Sample Operations Plan

The Readersville Bookshop will fill a void in the western downtown business district and adjacent residential area, and will promote itself as having a "great selection of books in hometown comfort." The store will be open from 10:00 a.m. to 7:00 p.m., accommodating diners from the next-door café and workers from local businesses. After several months of operation, hours may change according to the pattern of customer visits.

Readersville Bookshop plans to sell primarily used books. Sixty percent of these books will be paperback and 40 percent will be hardcover and collectibles. The Bookshop finances will be managed exclusively by the sole proprietor-owner, who will maintain the accounting statements, pay all bills, prepare tax reports, and purchase inventory and supplies.

The manager will be responsible for day-to-day operations, receiving and assessing books brought into the store by customers, issuing trading credit on the value of books accepted by customers, stocking the bookshelves, keeping inventory records of the books in stock and sold, assisting customers in locating out-of-print books, and accepting special book orders for customers. The manager will also be responsible for the hiring and training of temporary and part-time employees.

The Bookshop will operate as an active community partner in the Convention and Visitors Bureau, literacy projects, monthly art receptions, and school-business partnership activities.

3.5.8 Management and Staffing Plan

Who is your team and why will they be an asset in making your bookstore a fantastic success? This is the part of the plan to show potential lenders that you have put together a highly qualified group of people to help you run your bookstore.

Get out your resume, and the resumes of your team, and explain why you are winners. If you have not yet hired any staff, at least include information about yourself.

Before deciding how many employees to hire, consider the layout of your store and how easily and quickly employees can move across the floor to help customers. A small shop of 1,200 square feet all in one room may only need one full-time employee and one part-time employee for busy times and days when the full-time employee is off. However, a shop that size spread over two or three levels may require more. As an owner, you may also act as an employee when necessary.

3.5.9 Appendices

The appendices include all of the documents that support your claims. Any documents that you have prepared to show your financial capabilities should go here, as should completed loan applications, your team's resumes, and any materials that help you present your store. Use this section to show that you have done your homework and that the claims you make in the rest of the plan can be supported.

Five Important Planning Tips

Although business plans are mainly for getting funding, they also force you to do some important planning for your own knowledge, so don't skip this step. Donna Paz Kaufman of Paz & Associates has provided Five Planning Tips for New Booksellers below. Paz & Associates, The Bookstore Training & Consulting Group, is located online at **www.pazbookbiz.com**.

#1: Learn Before You Leap

People have a romantic idea about bookselling and they minimize the grit needed to open their own bookstores. When I see people stumble and fall as new booksellers, it is because they have not honored the bookselling business as the complex, unique business that it is. Learn about bookselling before you leap!

#2: Do Your Homework

Many times new booksellers will find what they believe is their perfect location before they have done any other planning. You need to plan for your store and have an accurate income statement and financial plan before you decide on a location. Occupancy expenses can't be decided upon before you determine the greater picture of what the potential revenue for the store is.

#3: Know Your Competitive Advantage

Know how you will be competitive and align your staffing and your marketing appropriately. For example, sometimes people say they will concentrate on customer service, or on their knowledge of books. When you say you are going to fulfill a mission of service, make sure you have the payroll to back up what it is you say you are going to accomplish. Also, align your marketing strategy and your competitive advantage. Decide who your market is — you can't be everything to everyone.

#4: Have Adequate Capital

Make sure you have the money to pull off what you are trying to do. You have to have the adequate capital to do what you want. Establish a budget that includes adequate funds for marketing. Often when booksellers are operating without enough capital, the first thing to go is the marketing budget. Without the proper marketing budget, the bookseller can't hope to succeed.

#5: Know Who Your Customers Are

You need to know who your customers are and work like crazy to keep them. And keep finding new customers. When you are a new bookseller, you need to introduce yourself to as many people as possible as quickly as possible and get them into your store. Getting people into the store is the only way you will be able to achieve your revenue targets.

4. Getting Ready to Open

As part of your planning you will need to consider a variety of matters related to opening your bookstore, such as:

- Whether to start a new store, take over an existing store, or open a franchise.

- How much start-up funding you will need and where you will get it from.

- Where your store will be located and how you will set it up inside.

- How to build and maintain your inventory.

Read on to learn about more things you'll need to consider.

4.1 Options for Opening a Bookstore

Maybe you've always dreamed of owning a bookstore. Maybe there is a strong need for a bookstore in your community, and those needs aren't being adequately met by the existing retailers. Or perhaps you've noticed a local bookstore for sale. You like it, and it's in a location that you know is a good one. You could buy it and operate it, taking advantage of its already established reputation and customer base.

Deciding which route is right for you is an important decision. An established, successful bookstore might cost more than starting from scratch, but it comes with customers, inventory, and reputation — which means it's likely to continue with its pre-established success.

A new bookstore typically costs less to start up, and you can tailor it specifically to your own vision. But you will need to spend lots on advertising, gaining clientele, and making a reputation for your business — and new businesses have a higher risk of failure.

4.1.1 Buying an Existing Bookstore

"New booksellers find bookstores in a myriad of ways. I found a "Bookstore for Sale" in the Business Opportunities Classified section of the daily newspaper. Since becoming a bookseller and a member of the Pacific Northwest Booksellers Association, I've read many times in our monthly newsletter about bookstores closing and seeking buyers. Bookstore owners retire, and that leaves the door open for new buyers."

— Pat Tegtmeier, A Novel View
Anchorage, Alaska

One way to become a bookseller a little more quickly than starting from scratch is to buy a pre-existing bookstore from another bookseller who, for whatever reason, is ready to get out of the business. When you buy an existing bookstore, consider these steps:

- Locating an existing bookstore that a bookseller is ready to sell that meets your expectations and your price range.

- Determining the type of purchase and what it includes.

- Working with the bookseller to complete the sales contract, which will include creating a business plan, seeking a business loan, and making sure the sale is legal and a wise investment by using your qualified attorney and accountant.

Finding a Previously Owned Bookstore

Just like Pat Tegtmeier did, you can begin your search for a bookstore in your local paper. You can also:

- Check out "For Sale" listings in your regional bookselling association trade paper or newsletter.

- Walk into bookstores that look interesting to you and ask the owner whether he or she is considering selling their store.

- Get the word out in your community with other booksellers that you are interested in buying an existing bookstore.

- Use the Internet to locate a potential bookstore for sale.

What Kind of Sale and How Much

Depending on the bookstore, and what exactly you agree to, purchasing a used bookstore will take as much financing as opening a new store. If you agree to buy all the existing stock (books, sidelines, all the fixtures, and so on) you will be purchasing the physical assets of the store. It is up to you to make sure in your agreement with the person selling the bookstore that you pay the current value for these assets.

According to Donna Paz Kaufman's booklet *Opening a Bookstore — An Introduction to Retail Bookselling*, a potential bookseller should expect an investment of up to $200,000 for a 2,000 square foot bookstore.

When considering buying a used bookstore, you will still need a similarly sizable investment. While you may not have to invest money to design or furnish the interior of your store, a bookseller selling their store to you will want to recoup a large portion of their original investment.

You will have to discuss each element of the transaction and agree on acceptable terms for things such as:

- Existing book stock

- Existing sideline stock

- Furnishings and fixtures

- Equipment

- Elements of the existing lease agreement

- Good will and reputation

Donna Paz Kaufman had this to say when asked about buying a used bookstore versus setting one up from scratch:

> "The best sources for information regarding resale bookstores for sale are the ABA (**www.bookweb.org**) and the regional booksellers association in the area a bookseller would like to live and work.

> Regarding how much you should pay for the purchase of a pre-existing or resale bookstore business, a lot depends on whether the bookstore is profitable, whether it has customer lists/loyalty programs, and its reputation in the local community and the book industry. I recommend only paying the current value of physical assets if the store is NOT profitable."

4.1.2 Franchising

Another way to own your own bookstore is to buy a franchise. A franchise is a good way to own your bookstore if you want to have the reputation and support of a large and established bookselling company. While this may not be for some booksellers who want to put their unique touch on everything they do and be completely in control of all their decisions, other potential booksellers will feel more comfortable getting involved in bookselling with a tried-and-true company.

What is Right for You

Before you make the decision to get involved with a franchise, make sure that you have thoroughly researched the franchise and that you are excited about and comfortable with all of the requirements and responsibilities of franchise ownership. Consider your reasons to explore a bookstore franchise. Perhaps you:

- Like the idea of owning your own bookstore but you would like the name and reputation of an established bookstore.

- Come from a corporate career and you like to have established rules and policies.

- Need help with the major aspects of opening your own store or you prefer not to do the legwork, research, and trial and error effort required to build your bookstore from the ground up.

- Want experienced people with expert knowledge to guide your process of opening your own bookstore.

A Word About Cost

John Glazer, CEO of Praxis Bookstore Group LLC/Little Professor Book Center, says that getting into a Little Professor Book Center franchise bookstore is practically comparable in cost to creating a start-up venture alone. For a Little Professor Book Center franchise, a 2,000 square foot space for a "Cadillac Operation" runs about $225,000 as compared to the figure of $200,000 noted by Donna Paz Kaufman.

Why the difference? In the case of the Little Professor Book Center franchise, a bookseller is paying for, and getting, what amounts to a full-time consulting service that helps them each step of the way with everything, including:

- Selecting your bookstore site

- Lease negotiation

- Financial planning and on-going support, including business plans and loan packages for start-up financing

- Marketing advice and support

- Inventory tools and assistance

- All-inclusive initial training

- Store opening organization

- Store layout and design

- Computer and technical support

- Fixture supply

- Internet services

- On-going training and support

For more information about Little Professor Book Center franchises, visit **www.littleprofessor.com**.

4.1.3 Opening a New Bookstore

Of course, you can always start from scratch and open a brand new bookstore. That way, you can have complete control over every step of the process and make sure that your shop is everything you want it to be. The next section will show you how to do just that.

4.2 Getting Started

So you dream about opening your own bookstore. This section explains how to go about turning that dream into a reality.

Protecting your interests, both personally and financially, is a very important part of opening your own bookstore. Before you open your bookstore, you will need to make sure that all the necessary legal requirements are handled. While you can get some advice from resources recommended in this guide, we advise you to consult with an attorney.

Because rules and laws vary depending on your location, it's also wise to get in touch with the nearest business development center. They'll help you gather all the information you'll need to get started, and walk you through the process of opening your business. Here are a few resources that offer helpful information as you start your own business.

The Service Corps Of Retired Executives has volunteers throughout the U.S. who donate time to mentor small businesses free of charge. Their site, located at **www.score.org**, has helpful articles.

The Small Business Administration is an excellent resource with advice on business licenses and taxes as well as general information on starting a business. You can also use the website to look up an SBA office near you. The site is located at **www.sbaonline.sba.gov**.

The Canada Business Service Center offers an Online Small Business Workshop which includes information about taxes, financing, incorporation, and other topics. You can also locate a nearby CBSC office through this website, at **www.cbsc.org/osbw**.

Nolo.com publishes legal information presented in plain English. Their Legal Encyclopedia at **www.nolo.com/lawcenter/ency/index.cfm** is an excellent resource.

You can also join a number of organizations designed for business owners to learn and network in an organized setting. One resource is your local chamber of commerce. Chambers usually have an annual fee and are set up to aid the local businessperson with a variety of business-related issues. Members attend local meetings and often take part in events designed to help them be more successful. To find out how to contact your local chamber, visit:

- *U.S. Chamber of Commerce Search Page*
  www.uschamber.com/chambers/chamber_directory.asp

- *The Canadian Chamber of Commerce*
  www.chamber.ca/article.asp?id=351

4.2.1 Choosing a Business Name

Choosing a business name is actually one of the most important things you can do to get ready to open your bookstore. The right business name will draw attention to your store and give potential customers a reason to walk through your door.

Steps in Determining Your New Bookstore's Name

Unfortunately, choosing a name isn't quite as easy as dreaming something up and saying, "That's it!" You have to make sure that no other business is operating with the same name, or a name similar enough that the owner sues you for detracting from their ability to do business. Here are some other things to consider when choosing a name:

Does It Say What You Want It To Say?

If you want to sell books, and you call your new bookstore "Steve's Stuff" or "The Store on Third Street," you could have a problem. Your bookstore's name will speak for your business when you aren't available to do so. Choose a name that lets people know what you do.

Is It Catchy?

Will people remember it? Is it attention-grabbing, or literary, or fun? Does it relate to your bookstore's niche or specialty? Pick a name that engenders interest, which is clever, or will appeal to your readers. Curiosity can catch customers!

Will People Remember It?

If you open a mystery bookstore called Sleuth's Nook, your customers will know exactly what you mean and they will, being mystery buffs, love the name. Naming it Bob's Book Barn might not bring to mind a well-stocked niche bookstore full of the best mystery books available. So, while Bob's Book Barn might be the perfect name for a bookstore somewhere, consider choosing a name that your mystery-buff customers will relate to and remember.

Do You Love It?

Ultimately, you are the person who will need to live with your bookstore's name. It should feel like it fits and it should make you happy.

Is It Based On Something That Could Change?

There are some things in life that you just can't control, so it is best to pick a name that won't be affected by unforeseen changes. For example, if you name your store 45th Street Books, you have to consider the idea that someday you might decide to relocate. If you name your store Only Mysteries, there might come a time that you increase your categories to include science fiction or fantasy — and your name will no longer reflect what you are trying to sell.

Many booksellers report that they change their categories based on what their customers prefer, or because their own interests change. How your bookstore evolves over time can impact your name. If your categories change, will your name still be relevant?

Is the Name Used by Anyone Else?

Naturally, you don't want anyone using your bookstore's name. You also want to make sure that the name you choose for your store is an original one. Once you decide on a name, search to see if it already exists somewhere else.

The first place to look is your local phone book, and then with your county clerk's office. If you are going to incorporate your bookstore, you will need to check your name with your Secretary of State's office to be sure that it hasn't already been taken. Once you register your name, it is protected from others using it. You can find contact information for the appropriate U.S. offices at **www.statelocalgov.net/index.cfm**.

In Canada, many companies offer an inexpensive name search service called NUANS (Newly Upgraded Automated Name Search). The government of Canada has information about this service at **www.nuans.com/ nuansinfo_en/index_en.htm**

Does the Name Infringe on Anyone's Trademark Rights?

If you are planning on calling your bookstore The Coca-Cola Bookstore, you had better think twice! The nice people at Coca-Cola won't like it because you will be infringing on their trademark rights. Coca-Cola is a registered trademark that has been associated with their carbonated beverage for years and only Coca-Cola has the right to use the name.

Many trademark names are pretty easy to spot, but just to be sure, do some research on the names you like. You can do an online search of the federal trademark database to determine whether a name has already been registered.

If you have the financial resources, you could hire a naming professional to help you choose the right name for your company. Known as name consultants or naming firms, these organizations are experts at creating names, and can help you with trademark laws.

> **TIP:** Business names don't have to be trademarked, but having them trademarked prevents anyone else from using the same name. Trademark laws are complicated, so if you think you want your company name trademarked it's a good idea to consult a lawyer with expertise in that area.

Most people starting a small business, however, don't have the money necessary to hire professional namers. The cost of these services can range from a few thousand dollars to upwards of $35,000. Some people get a group of friends together and brainstorm names. If somebody comes up with a really good one, you'll know it right away.

Filing Your Name

Unless the name you choose for your bookstore is your own name, you will have to file what is known as a DBA (Doing Business As) form or a fictitious business statement.

The details about how you file a fictitious business name vary from place to place, so it is best to call your local city or county clerk's office to check the requirements in your area. They will give you all the details, information about the associated costs, and let you know if you will need to have your fictitious business name published in your local newspaper.

For good advice on filing your name, trademarks and other matters to consider before choosing a business name, visit the links mentioned at the beginning of section 4.2.

4.2.2 Your Bookstore's Legal Structure

There are a variety of ways to set up the legal structure of your bookstore. They include:

- Sole proprietorship

- Partnership

- Corporation

- Limited liability company

Sole Proprietor

As a sole proprietor, you will be the sole owner of your business. Choosing a sole proprietership is probably the easiest way for a new bookseller to get started. However, as a sole proprietor you are personally responsible for all business liability. Some of the things you will need to do as a sole proprietor include:

- Getting all the necessary licenses required for opening your bookstore on a city, county, state, and federal level

- File the proper tax forms (see more in section 4.2.4 about taxes)

- File estimated taxes

- File a Doing Business As form if you are doing business as something other than your actual name

As a sole proprietor you can hire employees, but you need to remember that you are liable for anything an employee does. You will be responsible for filing the additional appropriate tax forms.

Additionally, it is important to make sure you are adequately insured. You are completely and personally responsible for all of the financial and legal obligations of your bookstore.

Forming a Partnership

Many bookstore owners decide to form the legal structure known as a partnership. Just as the name implies, a partnership means that you share the legal and financial responsibilities of your bookstore with one or more partners. This can be a very good thing because it allows you to share the cost of opening your new store.

However, there are also some associated risks. Whenever you deal with other people in a business context, you must make sure that they are honest and have the same ideas and objectives that you do.

You will need to have a partnership agreement that spells out every aspect of what you and your partners agree to do to open and run your new bookstore. It is a good idea to hire a reputable attorney to help you complete a partnership agreement and advise you about any important points you want to include to protect everyone involved.

To form a partnership, you will need to:

- Decide who owns what. You need to decide how you want to split ownership of the business. Sometimes you will not want a 50-50 split, but some other division of ownership.

- Decide who does what. You will need to discuss ahead of time who will be responsible for each aspect of the business.

- Decide who contributes what. What portion of the start-up and running costs will each partner be responsible for? The percentage of start-up monies invested is one way to determine the percentage of ownership of the bookstore.

- Decide who earns what. How much money will you and your partner take from the business for salary? How will this change over time based on profits?

- Decide who decides. What do you do if you can't agree? Are there some decisions that will be handled by one partner? How will you handle a disagreement about an important decision?

Limited Partnerships

Another way to work a partnership is called a limited partnership. If you wish to have complete responsibility for your bookstore, but you don't have the money to finance it, this might be a good option for you.

In a limited partnership, the general partner is the person who has the responsibility. A limited partner provides capital to finance the business.

There are laws that govern this kind of a partnership, and it is very important to check with your attorney to make sure your limited partnership follows the laws exactly. If you don't, you can end up with a regular partnership and not know it until a problem arises.

Corporation

A corporation is another legal structure that many booksellers choose for their businesses. A corporation has legal protections and benefits not found in other legal structures. Creating a corporation involves creating an entity that is not directly connected to your personal finances or wealth. In the case of lawsuit, the corporation is sued and not the individuals. In essence, you limit your personal liability. Many people choose to organize their business as a corporation for this very reason.

If you form a corporation, your business will have stock which you can sell to stockholders to raise capital. This is an excellent way to finance your business, but you have to decide whether or not you want to take on the additional responsibility of stockholders. If you sell stock, you are accountable to your stockholders.

In a privately held corporation, you and a small number of stockholders hold all the stock. If your corporation has more than 35 stockholders, then it becomes publicly held and will be subject to the rules and regulations of the government.

One important thing to note is that if you hold all your own stock, you can be personally liable for your company. Check with your attorney about the best way to set up your corporation to offer you the maximum protection and benefits.

To form a corporation, you need to:

- Get professional legal advice and help in filing not only the initial paperwork but also the necessary annual paperwork.

- Make sure you contact your business bank to set up a corporate account. The rules for corporate accounts differ from those for other business structures and personal accounts.

- Determine your reasons for incorporating, and decide if those reasons are worth the additional expense and time commitment required to set up and run a corporation.

Limited Liability Company

A limited liability company also is legally separate from the person or persons who own it, and offers some protections that a partnership does not.

Partners in a limited liability company get the same personal financial protection as those in a corporation. A limited liability company, however, can't sell stock or have shareholders or a board of directors.

Regulations regarding limited liability companies vary from area to area, so it's necessary to do your homework if you're interested in this sort of ownership. The resources at the start of this section have further information on business structures. Excellent advice is also offered at the Quicken website at **www.quicken.com/small_business/start**.

4.2.3 Business Licenses

Regardless of what form of legal structure you choose for your business, you'll need to obtain a business license.

This is not a difficult task. All it normally entails is filling out some forms and paying an annual license fee. Contact your city or county clerk's office for more information about registering your business.

Contact information can be found in your phone book or online through resources such as **www.sba.gov/hotlist/license.html**.

There may also be a number of other permits and licenses you will need:

- Retail businesses that collect sales must be registered with their state's Department of Revenue and get a state identification number. In Canada, you will need to register to collect the Goods and Services Tax.

- All businesses that have employees need a federal identification number with which to report employee tax withholding information.

- If you are putting up a new building for your bookstore, you will need appropriate permits. This is covered in section 4.4.2.

For information about local, state, and federal requirements, visit the resources mentioned at the beginning of section 4.2.

4.2.4 Taxes

While some people say the only sure things in this world are death and taxes, if you are properly informed and prepared you won't have to face your tax responsibility with a feeling of dread. In fact, once you are organized and you have enlisted the help of a good tax professional, taxes become just another regular bookstore task.

Get Informed First

The best thing you can do to make sure that you are aware of your tax obligation for your new bookstore is to inform yourself.

The Internal Revenue Service (IRS) has a number of informative documents online that you can look at today to learn the basics about everything you need to prepare for your taxes as a small business owner:

- *Small Business and Self-Employed One-Stop Resource*
  www.irs.gov/businesses/small/index.html

- *Tax Guide for Small Businesses*
  www.irs.gov/pub/irs-pdf/p334.pdf

For Canadian residents, the Canada Customs and Revenue Agency also provides basic tax information for new business owners.

- *Small Business and Self-Employed Individuals*
  www.cra-arc.gc.ca/tax/business/menu-e.html

It is also important to be informed about your tax obligation on a state and local level. Tax laws and requirements vary on a state-by-state basis and locally, too. Make sure that you find out exactly what you are responsible for in your state and city (don't forget about sales tax).

- *State Taxes*
  www.bankrate.com/brm/itax/state/state_tax_home.asp

- *Provincial Income Tax Comparison for Small Businesses*
  http://sbinfocanada.about.com/cs/taxinfo/l/aataxcomp1.htm

Getting Assistance

If you decide you prefer a qualified tax professional to help you handle your taxes, you will find you are in good company. Many booksellers decide to have a professional handle their taxes. However, just like any other aspect of your business, if you are informed about what you need, you can hire someone who is qualified to help you. Being informed about your tax obligations, even if you have someone else prepare your taxes, is simply good business.

4.2.5 Insurance

Before opening your bookstore, you'll need to ensure you have proper insurance coverage. Once you have opened your bookstore and it is stocked full of merchandise, you will want to protect it. Making sure you are properly insured is one excellent way to do that — and in the case of workers' compensation insurance, it is the law.

Types of Insurance

As you think about insurance, think about worst-case scenarios. For example, you must protect your business in case someone is injured in your store or in case of an emergency situation like a fire or a flood. You must also insure your employees. So for the basics you will need:

- Liability insurance

- Property insurance

- Workers' compensation insurance

Business Owner's Policies

For some small businesses, getting a Business Owner's policy is a good place to start. These policies are designed for small business owners with under one hundred employees and revenue of under one million dollars. They combine liability and property insurance together.

Small business owners like these policies because of their convenience and affordable premiums. You can find out more about these policies at the Insurance Information Institute website at **www.iii.org/ individuals/ business**.

The League of Independent Book Retailer Insurance Services (LIBRIS) is a subsidiary of the American Booksellers Association that offers an insurance program specifically tailored to independent booksellers. Find out more at **www.libris.org/booksellers/whatis.htm**.

Workers' Compensation Insurance

Most states in the U.S. have laws requiring small business owners to have workers' compensation insurance. This insurance provides coverage in case an employee is injured or falls sick on the job.

This sort of coverage is an absolute necessity in most states (with the exception of Texas) because it is law. Workers' compensation insurance protects your workers and ultimately your business.

Workers' compensation insurance is also mandatory in Canada, but the rules and regulations vary depending upon the part of Canada in which your bookstore is located.

Check out the following websites for more information:

- *Insure.com*
  (Click on "The Insure.com Workers Comp Insurance Law Tool")
  http://info.insure.com/business/workerscomp

- *Small Business Canada — Workers Compensation Insurance*
  http://sbinfocanada.about.com/cs/workerscomp

Insurance Benefits for Employees

Finally, you need to decide what sort of insurance benefits, if any, you would like to provide for your employees.

Depending upon the size of your bookstore and the amount of financing you bring to the table to begin with, this will vary. It's been proven that employees who receive benefits have more longevity on the job, and that jobseekers consider benefits to be very important in their search for long-term employment.

It's definitely worth a conversation with a reputable insurance agent to see what kind of insurance benefits you can provide, and if you can split the contribution with your employees to make it possible for them to have insurance benefits as part of their employment package.

4.3 Financing

Like Cuba Gooding, Jr., said in the film *Jerry Maguire*, someone has to "show you the money" before you can open your store. While you may have a small amount of personal savings to invest, chances are you will use at least one source of outside funding to start or grow your business.

This section covers figuring out how much start-up funding you'll need, where you can turn to get it, and what documents you'll need to apply for funding from a bank or lending institution. Additional advice on all aspects of financing your bookstore can be found at the Small Business Administration website at **www.sbaonline.sba.gov/financing**.

4.3.1 How Much You'll Need

Your biggest start-up costs will most likely be:

- Acquiring an inventory

- Expenses related to occupancy of the bookstore

Your inventory costs are related to obtaining a starting set of books and sidelines to sell. The amount this will cost you depends on how big your bookstore will be, and what type of books you plan to sell.

Obviously your initial expense to acquire used books will be less than if you buy all the latest best-sellers direct from the publishers. In general, you can expect your inventory to account for 40-50% of your total start-up costs. You can also use the formula explained below to estimate how much your product will cost you.

When leasing or buying an existing building, your costs may include deposits or down payments, renovations (materials and labor), decorating, furniture, equipment, signage, and fixtures. For a bookstore owner who is leasing or buying an existing building, occupancy costs will generally account for about 15-30% of your start-up expenses.

However, if you're building a new shop or planning extensive renovations, construction costs will bring occupancy expenses even higher. When estimating, include plumbing, electrical, carpentry, signage, and any other item that might be special to your concept.

In addition to inventory and occupancy costs, other significant start-up costs will come from advertising, supplies, insurance, professional services, and pre-opening (training) salaries.

Once your business is operating, your biggest expenses will probably be the occupancy expenses of rent, or monthly mortgage, and the associated utility costs; and salaries, along with the employer's contributions to the employees' Medicare, social security, unemployment and, in some cases, disability and health benefits.

Estimating Your Starting Inventory Cost

You can use the square footage of your selling space to estimate how much inventory you will have at any time to sell. Your "selling space" will be 90% of your shop's total square footage. A 1,200 square foot store, for example, has 1,080 square feet of selling space (90% of 1,200).

Fifty dollars per square foot is the average retail value of a bookstore inventory, so to estimate your inventory value, multiply your selling space by $50. This means that a store with 1,080 square feet of selling space has about $54,000 in retail inventory value. Your cost to acquire that amount will vary, but to help you be profitable it should not exceed 60%, or $32,400. You may also know specific reasons why this cost will be lower for you, such as purchasing existing inventory, or purchasing books in bulk at a low cost.

You can also use your anticipated annual revenue to calculate a beginning inventory. If you are buying an existing bookstore you can use actual figures to project what your annual revenue will be, but if you are starting from scratch, you will have to make an educated guess.

For an independent bookstore, the industry standard for annual revenues varies from about $100 to $500 per square foot of selling space. One hundred to one hundred fifty dollars is a conservative figure suitable for a bookstore just starting out, although once again you have to factor in your market and its nuances. By multiplying by these two conservative figures, the store with 1,080 square feet of selling space can roughly anticipate total annual revenues of $108,000 to $162,000. Let's use the higher amount for our example.

Once you have estimated your annual revenue, you will need to do some calculations using your expected inventory turnover — a healthy turnover in inventory is three times a year. If anticipated annual revenues are $162,000 and inventory turnover is three times a year, a bookstore will begin with an inventory of retail value roughly equal to one-third of $162,000.

In this case, starting inventory value in retail sales will be $54,000 (one-third of $162,000). Your purchase price should be 60% of that or less. At 60%, then, your inventory budget for the first four months of operation will be $32,400 (plus shipping).

Expect the Unexpected

You should add a cash reserve or contingency amount to your budget as a cushion for unexpected costs such as increased utility deposits or labor costs stemming from renovations or construction, changes in workers' compensation contribution rates, salary hikes, and other increases.

Many financial consultants think that having a nest egg to live on while you are starting up your bookstore is one of the most important things you can have. Some suggest at least six months' of living expense money — that is, all the money you will need monthly to pay all your personal living expenses, bills, and debts so you can focus on your new bookstore without stress.

Sample Start-Up Budgets

Two sample budgets are included below. The first budget outlines expenses incurred while buying an existing 1,200 square foot bookstore, while the second outlines expenses for starting a new bookstore of the same size. The six-month nest egg is not included in these budgets, but should be part of the money you have on hand or the amount you finance.

A) Buy Existing Bookstore (1,200 square ft.)

Start-Up Costs

Inventory (existing)	$ 20,000
Renovations	1,000
Furniture/Equipment	1,000
Professional services	1,000
Supplies	2,000
Deposits and fees	2,000
Salary	3,000
Training	3,000
Grand Opening advertising	2,000
10% cash reserve	3,500
Total:	$ 38,500

B) Start New Bookstore (1,200 square ft.)

Start-Up Costs

Inventory	$ 32,400
Renovations	20,000
Furniture/Equipment	20,000
Professional services	5,000
Supplies	5,000
Deposits and fees	3,000
Salary	3,000
Training	3,000
Grand Opening advertising	5,000
10% cash reserve	9,640
Total:	$ 106,040

Sample Operating Budget

When making your financial plan you also need to know your projected revenue and expenses. This will be an operating budget, and can be done weekly, monthly, annually, or over several years. If your business is just starting out, you'll have to estimate these figures.

When budgeting for staffing, keep in mind both the cost of salaries and the employer contributions you must make for each employee's Medicare, social security, and unemployment benefits. According to the U.S. Department of Labor Bureau of Labor Statistics, the national average annual wage in 2002 for a bookstore employee was $16,247, and the average weekly wage was $312. For a breakdown on the wages by state, see the NAICS classification number 45121 (for bookstores) at: **www.bls.gov/cew/ew02sect4445.pdf**.

Software and downloadable sample forms are available if you need help with itemizing these projections. One source for free downloadable forms is Entrepreneur.com at **www.entrepreneur.com/formnet**.

Operating Budget — New Bookstore (1,200 square ft.)

Estimated Revenue	$ 162,000
Less Cost of Goods Sold	97,200
Gross Profit	**$ 64,800**
Expenses:	
Wages	$ 20,000
Lease	15,000
Loan Payments	8,000
Advertising	2,500
Office Expenses	1,400
Utilities	3,600
Taxes and Fees	3,000
Total Expenses	**$ 53,500**
Net Profit (Gross Profit – Expenses)	**$ 11,300**

4.3.2 Preparing to Apply for Funding

Once you've developed your budget, and projected your expenses and income, you may discover that you're likely to come up short in meeting your projected expenses over the first year. This is when you should consider outside sources of funding, such as friends, family, business associates, or commercial lenders, to name a few.

Before you begin, you must prepare to approach these potential loan sources. They will want to see a business plan, financial projections, and a statement of your personal finances, as well as a statement of what other sources of start-up financing you will be using. You will have to include detailed listings of all your operating costs, including inventories, payroll, marketing, rent or mortgage, insurance, taxes, and utilities. Here are some of the key documents you will need when approaching lenders or investors.

Loan Fund Dispersal Statement

In this section you will break down the sources you think will be providing funding. As an example, $110,000 might come from $10,000 of your own savings; a $30,000 contribution from small investors, friends, and family; and a $70,000 bank loan secured by your home. Section 4.3.3 takes a look at possible funding sources for your business.

A Business Plan

As you learned in section 3.5, a business plan is the document that lenders will review, along with your personal finances, to decide whether to give you a loan. This document is absolutely necessary for banks or other lenders (even if it's just your rich aunt) so they can see that you have a clear and organized plan.

Financial Projections

Investors or lenders want to see that you can project being able to pay them back, with interest, in a reasonable amount of time, based on revenue and expense figures that have been researched and make sense. Your financial statements will include your start-up and operating budgets, as explained earlier, as well as a break-even analysis, and a projected profit and loss/income statement.

Break-Even Analysis

Your "break-even" is the sales you need to equal how much you are spending to run the business — also known as "breaking even." Once you are making sales past this point, your business starts to make a profit. Investors will want to see that you have an understanding of your break-even number, and that it is a reasonable one.

Once you have this figured out, you can then determine what kind of profit potential your bookstore has, as well as point out the need (and where) to control your costs. In most cases the numbers will work out fine. However, if they are just too out of line, then you need to re-organize around another possible location, a different type of inventory, or some other option that is more affordable.

Projected Profit and Loss/Income Statement

The income statement, or profit and loss statement, pulls together the other documents explained here and shows how much of a profit you plan to make over a period of time — quarterly, yearly, and sometimes for the next three to five years. (Don't show a loss, or you won't get the loan!) This section will contain spreadsheets that show the amount of money coming into and exiting your business. See the sample profit and loss statement on the next page for an example.

A Personal Financial Statement

You should prepare a personal financial statement as part of your business plan. If you are borrowing $50,000 or less, this will be the key document lenders consider when deciding whether to approve your loan. It will also give you a clear picture of your own finances, and let you know exactly where you are starting from. In this statement you will provide answers to these questions:

- How much money do you need every month to pay your bills?

- What kinds of resources or assets do you have?

- What kind of debt are you in? How will you repay this debt while you are putting your total effort into opening your store?

Sample Profit and Loss Statement

Income Projection: Year 1

Month	Income	Month	Income
Jan.	$ 12,500	Jul.	$ 14,000
Feb.	14,500	Aug.	15,500
Mar.	13,500	Sep.	11,500
Apr.	13,500	Oct.	13,500
May	13,500	Nov.	13,000
Jun.	13,000	Dec.	14,000
Total Sales			**$162,000**

Cost of Goods Sold

Month	Cost
January	$ 32,400
May	34,000
September	30,800
Total Cost of Goods Sold	**$ 97,200**

Expenses

Wages	$ 20,000
Lease	15,000
Loan Payments	8,000
Advertising	2,500
Office Expenses	1,400
Utilities	3,600
Taxes and Fees	3,000
Total Expenses	**$ 53,500**

Yearly Net Profit

Total Sales	$ 162,000
Total Cost of Goods Sold	97,200
Total Expenses	53,500
Yearly Net Profit	**$ 11,300**

You can download a sample financial planning form from Entre-preneur.com at **www.entrepreneur.com/formnet**. Under the menu, click on "Personal," then scroll down to "Personal Balance Sheet" and click on "Download this form."

Now that you know the basics, you are ready to determine who you will approach for your loan.

4.3.3 Sources of Start-Up Financing

You can use a mixture of the financing suggestions that follow. Many new booksellers choose to use some of their own savings, a family loan, and a small business loan. Only you can decide which financing sources will be the best ones for your business. The most important thing is to make sure you agree to loan payment terms that you can live with and that are realistic for you.

Commercial Loans

You can get commercial loans from a financial institution like a bank or a credit union. You can set up all your small business banking needs at the local bank around the corner, or you can shop around for a bank that will offer you the best loan terms possible.

Short-term loans of one year or less are commonly used to manage seasonal cash needs such as inventory purchases and accounts pay-able. Longer-term loans range from two to fifteen years, and are typically used to purchase real estate for your business.

In business loans, there are also two kinds of financing — equity and debt financing. Which one you choose will be based on the debt-to-equity ratio of your business — how much equity your business has, compared to how much debt it has. The more money you have invested, the easier it will be to get lenders to give you a loan.

The terms of your loan will depend upon several things:

- Your credit score

- Your collateral

- Your ability to pay back a loan

When applying for a commercial loan, you will need to prepare a loan proposal, usually by filling out a business credit application form provided by the lender. Expect to provide the following information:

- The type of loan you're applying for.

- Amount you're requesting.

- What you will use for collateral.

- How the money will be used.

- Information about your business, such as your name, address, phone, tax identification number, date established, legal structure, any other existing loans or lines of credit, taxes owed, or assets pledged.

- Details about the business owners or principals: name, housing payments, work information and salary, source and amounts of other income.

For a business that has ongoing credit needs ranging between $10,000 and $200,000, a credit line from a lender may be the way to go. The process is simple and approval generally takes only a few days. Once approved, the bookseller writes checks against the line of credit.

Personal Loans

One of the greatest resources for your start-up money will always be the people you know who believe in you and your ideas — your family and friends. They will help you with money when all other resources fail you. They usually will agree to payback terms that aren't as strict as commercial lenders, and they are usually pulling for you, too.

As with any other kind of loan, it is important to make sure that you and the other party both completely understand and agree to the terms of the loan. Also, make sure to put everything in writing.

Another possibility is to ask a family member to co-sign a commercial loan for you. Co-signing means that this person agrees to take on the financial responsibility of the loan if you should fail. Family members are often willing to help you out this way. Make sure, before friends or family members help you out by co-signing a loan, that they are really comfortable doing so.

Investors

Investors are looking to make money by investing in your business. They may or may not be people you know, but they will want to see how they will make a profit by helping you. You have to assure them that they will get something out of it, because for them, investing in your bookstore isn't personal, like it might be with a family member — it is business. Investors work one of two ways:

- They want to see their initial money returned with a profit.

- They want to own part of your business.

You have to decide what you want. Do you feel you will be able to meet the investor's terms? Do you want to share ownership of your business with another person? For some new bookstore owners, the perfect solution is to find a partner, share the responsibility of their new bookstore, and bring some money to invest.

Government Programs

Small Business Administration (U.S.)

The Small Business Administration (SBA) doesn't actually lend you money. What they do is guarantee a loan that a commercial lender will give you. In essence, the SBA gives lenders the reassurance that they will pay back the loan if you don't. They provide the extra assurance that many lenders need to "show you the money."

But the SBA must be convinced that your loan is a good risk, and you must apply for an SBA loan in order to access these commercial lenders. You can read more about the process at the SBA link given at the beginning of this section.

The SBA has an excellent division aimed at women, called the Office of Women's Business Ownership. While their website (which is located at

www.onlinewbc.gov) is geared toward women, the advice and practical information is some of the best available anywhere and is valuable for every new bookstore owner. One especially important section of their website is the Finance section (**www.onlinewbc.gov/docs/finance**), which gives step-by-step instructions on almost every financial aspect of opening a new business.

Business Development Bank (Canada)

"In Canada, we have the Business Development Bank, a federal institution that provides funding when other resources are not available, but at a higher rate of interest."

— Suzanne Brooks, President
Canadian Booksellers Association

If you are planning to open a bookstore in Canada, you can learn more about the Business Development Bank of Canada and its financing resources at **www.bdc.ca/en/home.htm**.

You

Never forget that you might be your own best source of funding. Bookstore owners commonly use their own money as an initial investment in the business, and this follows the pattern for small business start-ups in general. According to Entrepreneur.com, 67 of the "Hot 100" companies of 2004 used savings or personal funds to finance their start-ups.

One nice thing about using your own money is that you aren't beholden to anyone else or any other organization — it is yours to invest. This can be an excellent solution for individuals with some credit problems. To raise your own capital, you can:

- Cash out stocks, bonds, life insurance, or an IRA.

- Increase your credit on charge cards.

- Use savings.

- Take out a second mortgage on your house or other property.

- Sell something valuable, like a car, jewelry, real estate, or art.

4.3.4 Real-Life Financing Examples

To get an idea of what sources of funding booksellers typically use, we asked three booksellers how they funded their bookstore, and what they considered to be the advantages or disadvantages of the route they took. Here's what they shared.

Bookstore A

This small independent used bookstore in the Northwest U.S. opened in 2001 in a leased building, financed by the owner's personal retirement funds of $32,000. The major advantage is that the bookstore has no debt and pays all bills on time. The downside is that growth is restricted and funds for marketing are limited.

Bookstore B

The owner of this bookstore in the Midwest U.S. started without a retail space, selling through displays at antique shows and private sales. Hard work, frugality, and honest bookkeeping helped him secure a line of credit from his longtime bank. Eventually a building was purchased, and this company now operates three stores and a warehouse, with more than one million volumes and 80,000 square feet.

Bookstore C

This mid-sized independent bookstore in the Western U.S. began as a very small store in 1974. The owners secured a $500 loan from a family member and another $500 loan from a large bank, co-signed by the same family member.

The owners got a $10,000 SBA loan through the same bank in 1978 to expand to 1,800 square feet. In 1983, when expanding to 5,000 square feet, the owners borrowed $20,000 on a conventional loan from a small bank. In 1988, the store moved to a 12,667 square foot location with a $400,000 loan from a larger bank (with SBA guarantee) and $75,000 from a family member.

As of this writing, the outstanding bank and personal loans are about $95,000. The store's owners say that borrowing from family is more flexible, but that the funds are limited and there are certain personal stress factors involved. They consider it good fortune that their largest loan had a floating interest rate that dropped in half over the life of the loan.

4.4 Physical Store

Look at potential locations for your store, or at least think about what part of town might be the right location. Once you find a potential location for your store, you still have a lot to do. You will need to:

- Find out if the space you want is available.

- See if the lease terms for the space work for you.

- Meet the landlord. Determine whether you can see yourself having a happy working relationship with them.

- Make sure you like the "feel" of the place. Find out if it has everything you need and how much it will cost you.

- Sign the lease.

- Research, select, and buy all your equipment and inventory.

- Set up shop!

4.4.1 Finding a Space

Finding a space that suits you can take a little work, but once you have the perfect location, the thrill of opening your own bookstore will be that much closer!

You probably have some idea about where you envision your bookstore's location and what sort of a space you are looking for. But to make sure that you don't get stuck with something you are unhappy with, be as definite as possible about all the particulars you are looking for in a space before you begin your search. Use the following idea list to begin your brainstorming process:

- In what part of town would I like to locate my bookstore?

- Are there any other independent bookstores nearby?

- Are any nearby bookstores similar enough in concept to my store to be direct competition?

- Are any superstore or large chain bookstores close to the area where I would like to locate my store?

- Are there any obviously empty storefront locations that appeal to me?

- Are there any other buildings that might prove to be an interesting home for my store?

- Have I checked local malls or strip malls?

- Have I observed car traffic near my store at different times of the day?

- Have I found a place for my store that has a lot of foot traffic, pedestrians, commuters, or tourists?

- Have I determined what other businesses are in the area? Are there restaurants, coffee shops, movie theaters, or other businesses that might attract customer traffic to my store?

- Is the area that I am considering safe and comfortable? Would customers think so?

As you begin to consider what you need in a space, think about three things:

- Things you must have

- Things you would like to have

- Things that you definitely want to avoid

Must Haves

When you are considering the perfect space for your bookstore, what are the things you must have? To begin with, there is undoubtedly a limit to the amount of rent you will be able to pay monthly for your lease. Consider exactly how much rent you are willing to pay, and figure out the highest price your business budget allows for monthly lease costs.

Other "Must Haves" might include a good neighborhood, a place with excellent public transportation or freeway access, or a space with quiet neighbors. Just imagine a bookstore with a dance academy upstairs, or a bookstore above a delicatessen that sells smoked meats. Neighbors can definitely affect your customers' ability to enjoy your bookstore. Because of this, neighbors who don't detract from the overall experience of your bookstore are a must have.

Nice to Haves

"Nice to Haves" are the elements or features about a space that would add to the overall attractiveness of your space, but that you could live without if necessary. Some things that might be nice could include an exterior with a garden area or a place for outdoor benches, a store location near a place where pedestrians cross, or close proximity to a coffee shop or bakery. (This could be a thing to avoid if one of your pet schemes is to open your own café as part of your bookstore.)

Things to Avoid

As you consider what you want in a space, some things will come up that are important for you to avoid. For example, if you choose a space that has a shared ventilation system with the pet store next door, and you happen to be allergic to cats, you will live to regret the day you signed your lease. Naturally, any space right next to a competing bookstore, or a building slated for demolition next year, would be something to avoid. It is very important to find out as much as you can about any potential space before ever considering a commitment.

Keeping Track of Places You've Seen

As you look at properties for the perfect potential space for your new bookstore, keep track of where you have been, what each potential space looked like, and the positives and negatives of each space. Consider taking along a Polaroid camera on your space-hunting trips to take a picture of each space's exterior and interior so you can remember the details later.

To make the process easier, use the checklist provided on the next few pages for each of your space hunting excursions. This checklist, along with a picture or two, will help you to be really clear about each potential location you visit so you can make an informed decision.

Finding Your Perfect Space Checklist

Date: _____

Location: _____

Pictures

❑   Exterior front

❑   Interior

Notes on pictures:

_____

_____

Space Location Checklist

1.   Does the space have easy freeway access?   *Yes No*

2.   Does it have handy public transportation?   *Yes No*

Where and what?

_____

_____

3.   Is the quality of the neighborhood good?   *Yes No*

4.   What possibly helpful businesses are nearby?

_____

_____

5.   What possibly detrimental businesses are nearby?

_____

_____

Exterior Checklist

1.   How is the overall appearance of the building exterior?

_____

_____

2.   Does it need any obvious work?   *Yes No*

What?

_____

_____

3.   Is the building a storefront location?   *Yes No*

4.   Is there a garden or parking strip area?   *Yes No*

Who maintains it? _____

5.   Where is the trash area?

_____

_____

6.   Is trash pickup included as part of the lease   *Yes No*
     agreement?

7.   Is the tenant responsible for:

Sidewalk maintenance?   *Yes No*

Shoveling snow?   *Yes No*

General cleanup of trash and debris?   *Yes No*

Interior Checklist

1.   How is the overall appearance of the building interior?

_____

_____

2.   Does it need any obvious work?   *Yes No*

What?

_____

_____

3.   What is the square footage of the space?   _____

Is there any room to grow?   *Yes No*

4. Are the windows functional? *Yes No*

5. Are there enough windows? *Yes No*

6. Is there adequate light? *Yes No*

7. Are the air conditioning and heating systems shared or private for each tenant? _____

8. Is the ventilation system shared or private for each tenant? _____

9. Is the space technology-ready? *Yes No*

10. Will you be able to use your existing Internet *Yes No* Service Provider if you have one?

11. Is the space wired for cable modem or DSL? *Yes No*

12. Is the space wired for phone lines? *Yes No*

    How many? _____

13. Does the space have private or shared restroom facilities? _____

14. What is the overall state of the existing restroom facilities? _____

15. Are there separate facilities for men and women? *Yes No*

16. Does the space have hot and cold running water? *Yes No*

17. Are there existing janitorial services? *Yes No*

    Is the cost for this service part of the lease price? *Yes No*

18. Does the space have a workroom or break room? *Yes No*

19. Does the space have a kitchen? *Yes No*

Extra Charges

1. What services and utilities are included in the lease price?

    _____

    _____

2. What services and utilities are provided by the landlord for a fee?

    _____

    _____

3. What services and utilities are the responsibility of the tenant?

    _____

    _____

Shared Tenant Spaces, Costs, Responsibilities

1. What spaces are shared with other tenants, if any?

    _____

    _____

2. What responsibilities are shared with other tenants, if any?

    _____

    _____

3. What costs are shared with other tenants, if any?

    _____

    _____

4. Is there a mandatory tenant association?   *Yes No*

Extra Benefits and Features

1. What extra benefits or features make this space especially desirable?

    _____

    _____

    _____

4.4.2 Signing Your Lease

Signing a lease for your bookstore space is quite a bit more than putting your signature at the bottom of a legal document. There are a variety of different lease options you can have and a number of things to consider when putting together the details in your lease.

What to Include In a Lease

Your lease is the legal agreement that makes it clear what each party will do (or won't do). Therefore it is vital that you get everything you expect regarding your bookstore space written into the lease. For example, once you have located a space you really like there still may be a number of improvements that you want to have happen before you move in.

Regular Improvements

Regular improvements are the things that a landlord will do for any prospective tenant — no matter what their business. These are the things that need to be done to prepare the space. Some of the things you should expect (although you should check just to be sure) include:

- Having the space prepared and cleaned by a professional janitorial service

- Painting the interior or exterior of the building as part of normal wear and tear

- Replacing worn bathroom fixtures, mini blinds, or broken fixtures

- Replacing worn or damaged carpet or flooring

Specific Improvements Requests

Specific improvements are the things you want to see done to your space to make it the way you dream it should be. This might include:

- Adding partitions

- A kitchen area for a café

- Installing a door or a window

- Creating storage or office space

- A break room for employees

In short, these improvements are the things you might hire a contractor to do.

Based on the term of your lease (a longer-term lease makes a landlord more willing to help fund improvements), your landlord will need to agree to the specific improvements that you want to make to the space and all of this will need to be included in the lease agreement. You must determine what the landlord will let you do, what the landlord will fund, what you will need to fund, and who will do the work.

> **TIP:** If the space you are considering needs too many improvements, maybe you haven't found the right space. Consider looking for a space that fits more of your needs before you commit to a long or complicated improvement plan.

Permits and Other Requirements

Permits

If you are going to make improvements to your space, you will need to make sure that you check your local city, county, and state regulations and get the proper permits to proceed.

Also, if you are considering opening a café or restaurant that serves food as part of your bookstore, you will need to contact the health department.

Zoning

Another thing to ask your potential landlord is whether or not the space you are considering renting is zoned as a retail space (and, if you are considering adding food to your store, as a café).

The difference between zoning and the need for a permit is relatively simple. Zoning indicates where a business can set up and permits designate whether a business can operate.

Handicapped Access

Also, as part of the Americans with Disabilities Act, businesses are required to provide handicapped access. Make sure to discuss this with any landlord you are considering renting space from. You can find out more about the Americans with Disabilities Act at **www.usdoj.gov/crt/ada/adahom1.htm**.

Types of Leases

First you will need to consider the type of lease that will work best for your store. Your lease will most likely fall into one of these categories:

Month-to-Month Lease

A month-to-month lease is the most flexible kind of lease agreement you can have. If you think you might want to get out of your lease quickly, all that is necessary to do so is 30 days notice.

Naturally, there is a downside to this sort of a lease. With a month-to-month lease, you aren't locked into a price for a reasonable length of time, plus the landlord can ask you to leave with 30 days notice.

Short-Term Fixed Rate Lease

While a short-term fixed rate lease has all the benefits of a shorter month-to-month lease, it also locks you into a fixed price for the length of the lease. This sort of commitment might be wise if you are truly concerned about giving up your current job to open your bookstore and want a short amount of time to see if it will really work.

With a short-term lease, you can add verbiage in the lease to determine what happens after the lease ends. What happens next is up to you and the landlord to negotiate.

Long-Term Lease

A long-term lease is a lease with a term of a year or more. Long-term leases that are for several years or even longer are called "multi-year leases." The best thing about a long-term lease is that once you find a great space, you can stay there for as long as you want.

Leases and the Art of Negotiation

Some booksellers don't realize that a lease document prepared and presented by a potential landlord is a negotiating tool. You certainly don't have to accept the terms of a lease you are uncomfortable with, and you can negotiate for the things you would like to see both added to and removed from the lease.

The lease written by a landlord is written in the landlord's best interests, not yours, so look for what you feel needs to be changed or amended to make the lease fit your requirements. Remember, the process of signing a lease is a negotiating experience. Both you and your landlord will probably need to bend a little to come up with a document that works well for both of you.

Don't feel pressured into signing a lease as soon as it is handed to you. Plan on taking the document away with you so you can read it carefully, and, if you wish, show it to a qualified attorney for advice. Good advice on leasing can be found at the links mentioned at the beginning of section 4.2.

4.4.3 Interior Design

Interior design is really one of the most enjoyable parts of opening your own bookstore. There is nothing like planning and preparing for your store, and then suddenly seeing it ready, in all its glory, just waiting for the first customer to step through the door. Planning your space helps you create an environment that customers will love and enjoy being in. Creating a space that customers love will encourage them to buy — and to return again.

There is a saying that "form follows function." And when space planning for your bookstore, this saying is true. Before you decide on what you will have in your store – the furniture, the fixtures, the equipment, and the supplies – you must decide how you want each area of your space to function.

After you decide how each area must function, you can decide the form that the space will take. You will choose the personality of your bookstore, and how that will translate into design, décor, and furnishings.

You will create an atmosphere, a color scheme, and possibly even a theme to give your bookstore an overall look that makes a statement. Design creates an experience for customers. The appearance of your bookstore will affect the way people feel about being in it.

To design the interior space of your bookstore, imagine your bookstore full of customers. Ask yourself:

- What are their needs?

- What are their expectations?

- What sort of design elements will they need to move through your door, enjoy the process of shopping in your bookstore, and have a positive experience purchasing what they want?

- How can you set up a functional store interior that will help them get what they want and leave, happily anticipating their next return trip?

The Practical and the Aesthetic

Making your space work requires attention to how the space functions effectively to help both you and your customers accomplish your objectives (the practical) and how it looks and feels to customers and to you (the aesthetic). In the most successful and memorable bookstores, owners figure out a creative way to meet both the practical and aesthetic needs for their customers and themselves.

To begin with, what do you want people to do in your store? Ultimately, you want them to buy books and other merchandise. But let's take a look at some potential customer objectives and consider how each area of your bookstore's space will need to function to be a success.

As you consider each space, think about how practical and aesthetic considerations will make each space work as well as possible. For example, let's look at how to fulfill a customer's need to feel welcome and have their questions answered in each of the following areas:

Space Solution Need and Area Chart

The Need	The Solution
Feel welcome and have their questions answered	Entrance and information area
Browse for books and sidelines	Fixtures and displays; shelf areas
Find the books they want	Fixtures and displays; shelf areas
Discover books that they didn't know about before	Displays and feature displays
Read and relax	Seating areas
Read and relax with children	Children's reading area
Socialize	Café; community room
Enjoy a cup of coffee and a light snack	Café
Listen to music or books on tape to make selection	Music or books on tape listening station
Attend events, book clubs, and discussion groups	Community or presentation area or room
Use a restroom	Restroom area
Make a phone call	Public telephone area
Use an Internet or wireless modem connection	Internet jacks; a WiFi signal; seating for laptop users
Wait while their loved ones or friends shop or browse	Waiting area
Request special services to accommodate disabled customers	Handicapped entrance; bathrooms; large-print book section

Your Sign

The Practical

Sometimes referred to as "signage," the sign in front of your store may be the very first indication to a customer that your bookstore exists.

On a practical level, your store's sign must be large enough to be read, not obstructed by anything else, and in good repair. A lighted sign with several lights burned out doesn't make a good first impression. Neither does a sign that is partially obscured.

If your location comes with a place to install a sign (such as in a shopping mall), you will probably be able to order an appropriate sign with the help of the mall's management. Professional sign companies offer design and manufacturing — check in your local Yellow Pages under the "Signs — Commercial" category.

Before deciding on a sign for your bookstore, check with your landlord and the city to find out if there are any special requirements or rules to take into consideration before you can select the perfect sign for your bookstore. Some places have rules that determine size, placement or look of signs. Make sure your chosen sign meets these standards by taking the design and description to the municipal office.

The Aesthetic

Your sign is the first place where you can express the personality and the character of your bookstore. The design, the colors, the words used in the name of your bookstore — all of these help you set the tone about what sort of a place your bookstore is. If you are going for a hip college look, your sign will be far different than if you are creating a sign for an upscale bookstore aimed at attracting seasonal tourists.

How creative your bookstore's sign is will be determined by the regulations that your city has about signs. Some cities are very lenient and others are amazingly strict. Even with strict guidelines, the right lighting, materials, and style of lettering can help you convey personality.

The Sidewalk and Front Door Area

The Practical

The sidewalk and front door area of your store exist for one reason: to get customers in your store. Some bookstores use outside displays of sale books. (Consider ordering publisher's overstock books — they are beautiful and eye-catching, but still a cost-effective choice.) These should be easy to access, and at table height. It is important for you to see the area and your merchandise from inside the store to prevent theft. It also helps draw potential customers in if they can see inside.

> **TIP:** An outside front door area book display won't work in every climate. Consider the weather and time of year to determine the best time to have an outdoor display.

The Aesthetic

The whole purpose of an outside display of sales books is to hook customers emotionally and make them feel like coming into your store will be fun, interesting and personally rewarding. Your outside display shouldn't be made of old books that you think are horrible but you are praying someone will buy. Display something trendy or familiar, something for kids, something wonderful and colorful, something great for a present — and make sure they are great deals.

The Windows

The Practical

Your window areas are probably your best opportunity to create onsite marketing and promotions for your bookstore. Many booksellers spend a lot of time changing their window displays and hooking these displays to holidays, new best-sellers, or upcoming in-store events. On a practical level, your window is instant advertising for your bookstore.

The Aesthetic

Create a feeling or a mood with seasonal, holiday, and special event window displays when decorating your windows. Interesting colors and vivid displays will help you pull people into your store. Frequently changing your displays can really attract attention.

The First Step In

The Practical

When thinking about the first step in the door, one longtime bookseller said, "I have about two seconds to catch my customer and get them to actually walk in my store once they open the door. What I have directly in front really determines if I can get customers to come in." What you place directly in view as a customer steps in is vital. Make sure your feature display is placed directly in the line of sight of entering customers.

The Aesthetic

A feature display should jump out and hook you. Think color, think new and interesting — try to imagine the hottest topic, trend or new book that your customers will be after and design your front feature display to grab their attention.

The Information Area

The Practical

An information area – even if it is also your cash wrap area – needs to be functional. It should have a computer where staff can look up book information for customers. It's also a good idea to have flyers for upcoming author appearances and signings, newsletters, and complete information about upcoming in-store events.

The Aesthetic

It's a helpful idea to label the information area with a sign so people are sure they are asking for information in the right place. And, although not necessarily a design element, it is important that staff working in this area be polite, welcoming, and willing to answer questions.

What to Do Next

Now take a look at all the different "space solution" areas of your store in the chart on page 157 and brainstorm about what practical and aesthetic needs each will have. Use the Setting Up Shop Form on the next page as an example to help you think.

Sample Setting Up Shop Form

The Need:

Safe and enjoyable place for children to use in store.

The Space Solution:

Well-designed children's area that is attractive, well-made, and safe for children, but still accommodates parents comfortably for maximum family enjoyment.

Space Element #1: The Shelves

Practical: The shelves must be completely secure and well-made so they will absolutely not fall over even if a child should climb on one.

Aesthetic: The shelves should be inviting, allow for a lot of face-out placement of books so children can see the beautiful artwork of picture books.

Space Element #2: Overall Area Design Elements

Practical: Everything should be sized for childen, like the tables and chairs. There should be no cords or open outlets so children will not get hurt.

Aesthetic: Extra large stuffed animals should grace the tops of the short shelves. There should also be fun seating choices like bean bag chairs and a story-time rug.

Space Element #3: The Reading Area

Practical: Must accommodate at least 10 children sitting in a circle and a reader in a chair in the front. Should have a large container with a safety lid, or no lid, for puppets and props and things that children can use to act out the story.

Aesthetic: Should be colorful and inviting. Decorations should have a castle and knights theme like fairy tales. Consider a large cartoon-friendly dragon on the wall?

4.4.4 Equipment and Supplies

Now that you have thought through the practical and aesthetic features of design, you are ready to think about choosing the functional pieces of equipment, fixtures, and supplies to make your store's design take shape.

This section begins with suggestions for each area of the store, followed by information about suppliers. Chapter 5 on store operations has additional advice on computer equipment and supplies.

Suggestions for Each Area

By using the areas you determined as "space solutions" in the previous section, you can easily organize all the equipment and supplies you need into categories based on these areas in your bookstore. Here are some suggested equipment and supply ideas for each "space solution area" to get you started:

TIP: A good rule of thumb is to budget for $10 to $20 per square foot of selling area.

Equipment and Supplies Checklist

Bookshelves and Fixtures

- ❏ Shelves

- ❏ Fixtures

- ❏ Category signs

- ❏ Step ladder for out-of-reach books

Cash Wrap Area

- ❏ POS cash register

- ❏ Computer system

- ❏ Counter area

- ❑ Phones
- ❑ Credit card machines
- ❑ Computer
- ❑ Bags and wrapping supplies
- ❑ Pens, scissors, tape
- ❑ Gift boxes and wrapping paper
- ❑ Business cards
- ❑ Bookmarks
- ❑ Gift certificates
- ❑ Receipt tape for register

Displays and Feature Displays

- ❑ Tables
- ❑ Seasonal tie-in sidelines
- ❑ Book tie in sidelines
- ❑ Co-op advertising display packs
- ❑ Publisher displays

Seating Areas

- ❑ Chairs
- ❑ Tables
- ❑ Reading lamps
- ❑ Overhead lighting

Children's Reading Area

❏ Beanbag chairs

❏ Child-size tables and chairs (sturdy enough for adults to use, too)

❏ Extra large stuffed animals for displays

Café

❏ Kitchen supplies and equipment

❏ Display case for pastries

❏ Coffee maker and grinder

❏ Cappuccino machine

❏ Restaurant supplies

❏ Cash register

❏ Counter area for cash register and payment

❏ Chairs

❏ Tables

Music or Books on Tape Listening Area

❏ Listening stations

❏ Headphone sets

❏ Chairs

❏ CD display racks

❏ Feature display tables

Community Room or Presentation Area

- ❏ Screen

- ❏ Tables

- ❏ Chairs

- ❏ White board with pens and erasers

- ❏ Internet jacks or WiFi (wireless remote Internet access)

- ❏ Podium for stage area

- ❏ Overhead projector

- ❏ Traditional slide projector

- ❏ Computer projector

- ❏ Coffee pot and supplies

- ❏ Microphone and amplifier

- ❏ Microphone stand

Restroom Area

- ❏ Infant and toddler changing station

- ❏ Paper supplies

- ❏ Soap and other restroom supplies

- ❏ Janitorial supplies

- ❏ Mop

- ❏ Broom

Public Telephone Area

❑ Pay telephones

❑ Local phone books

❑ Chairs

❑ Notepads

❑ Pencils or pens

Internet Hookup Area for Customers

❑ Modem jacks

❑ WiFi equipment

❑ Tables

❑ Chairs

❑ Appropriate lighting for computer use

Waiting Area

❑ Comfortable chairs

❑ Tables

❑ Magazines

❑ Access to coffee or water

Handicapped Areas

❑ Floor aisles wide enough for wheelchairs

❑ Wheelchair ramps

❑ Wheelchair elevators if steps are present

❑ Rails in handicapped restroom

Break Room

- ❏ Tables
- ❏ Chairs
- ❏ Refrigerator
- ❏ Microwave
- ❏ Time clock
- ❏ Trashcans
- ❏ Bulletin board for employee laws and other postings
- ❏ Coffee maker and coffee supplies

Office

- ❏ Printer
- ❏ FAX machine
- ❏ Copier
- ❏ Computers
- ❏ Computer printers
- ❏ Desks
- ❏ Chairs
- ❏ Filing cabinets
- ❏ Phones
- ❏ Answering machine
- ❏ Office supplies
- ❏ Letterhead, envelopes and business cards
- ❏ Software

Warehouse/Shipping Area

❑ Large tables

❑ Heavy shelving for large boxes

❑ Shipping tape

❑ Computer

❑ Printer

❑ Fax machine

❑ Phones

❑ Filing cabinets

❑ Bubble wrap

❑ Invoice and other shipping forms

❑ Shipping labels

Overall Store

❑ Paint

❑ Wallpaper

❑ Mini blinds

❑ Window treatments

❑ Wall decorations

❑ Carpeting or area rugs

❑ Cleaning supplies

❑ Air filters

❑ Light bulbs

❑ Broom, mop, and vacuum cleaner

Suppliers

General Business Supplies

Office supplies are easy to find and can be purchased at a variety of locations. Staples and Office Depot are competitively priced, and may deliver if you buy in quantity.

Retail Supplies

To find supplies used specifically for retail (such as bags, gift certificates, etc.) you can check the Yellow Pages or do an online search for retail supplies. Here are a few suppliers to get you started.

- *NEBS*
  www.nebs.com

- *VeriPack*
  www.veripack.com

- *Shopping Bags Direct*
  www.shoppingbagsdirect.com

Retail Fixtures

To find shelves and fixtures for displaying books, you can check the Yellow Pages or do an online search for retail fixtures.

One example to get you started is Franklin Fixtures, located at **www. franklinfixtures.com**. Yahoo has a directory of suppliers at **http://dir. yahoo.com/Business_and_Economy/Business_to_Business/ Retail_Management/Fixtures**.

To save on the cost of store fixtures, here are some ideas from Lori Soard, author of the *FabJob Guide to Become a Secondhand Store Owner*:

> "Often you can find used display cases through local newspaper classifieds. Be on the lookout for stores going out of business — do not be afraid to approach them and offer to purchase their display fixtures. You might also consider building the fixtures yourself or hiring someone to do so."

Cash Registers

As with other types of equipment, there are a number of places you can find cash registers. The Cash Register Store (**www.cashregisterstore. com**) is a good source for new registers, while eBay (**www. ebay.com**) is a good place to find them used.

> **TIP:** Before purchasing a cash register, make sure you have looked into what type of software you will be using to process your sales as it may need to tie in with your cash register. Section 5.2.1 covers computer equipment, including software.

Café Supplies

If you have a café in your bookstore, you can find supplies by doing a search for restaurant supplies or coffee wholesalers. Here are a few suppliers recommended by Tom Hennessy, author of the *FabJob Guide to Become a Coffee House Owner:*

- *EspressoPeople*
  www.espressopeople.com
  Phone: (888) 280-8584

- *KaTom*
  www.katom.com
  Phone: (800) 541-8683

- *Superior Products*
  www.superprod.com
  Phone: (800) 328-9800

- *Rapids*
  www.4rapid1.com
  Phone: (800) 899-6610

4.5 Inventory

Without a doubt, the most important items you will purchase for your bookstore are books. This section begins by looking at where to buy your inventory, including new books, used books, remainder books and sidelines. It then gives you advice to help you decide which books to buy for your store. By the end of this section, you will be ready to start planning for and buying your bookstore's inventory.

4.5.1 Buying from Publishers and Wholesalers

If you are selling new books, you will buy your inventory from publishers and wholesalers. You will need to develop a working relationship with a sales rep from any publisher or wholesaler you regularly order books from. You will find that these people can really provide an ordering support network for you and help you find what you need, especially when you are starting out.

Buying From Publishers

A publisher's sales rep can help you buy frontlist books (newly released titles) as well as midlist books (new titles that are expected to sell more moderately). Publishers will usually be able to sell to you at a bigger discount or lower cost than wholesalers. Additionally, publishers sales reps can often help you to get co-op money, which is money that publishers set aside to help booksellers advertise selected books.

According to an article published by *Publishers Weekly* in June 2003, following are the five largest U.S. publishers:

Random House

Website: **www.randomhouse.com/bookseller**

The Random House website has a special link for booksellers that includes information about titles, ordering information, a consumer catalog, information about terms of sale and even a downloadable file giving information about remainder books by season. You can also sign up for an email newsletter called "Bookseller Confidential" which provides booksellers with information about books, reviews, and other insider information to help you make informed book-buying decisions.

Penguin

Website (U.S.):   **http://us.penguingroup.com**
Website (Canada): **http://booksellers.penguin.ca**

The Penguin Group's website has different features, depending on whether you're in the U.S. or Canada. Browse the sites and see what Penguin has to offer. (If you're trying to look at the Canadian site, you must first complete a short – but free – online registration form.) Then, if you're interested in setting up a retail account with them, call (800) 847-5515 to talk to a sales rep.

HarperCollins

Website: **www.harpercollins.com/hc/readers/tool.asp**

HarperCollins has created several tools to make buying from them easier and more efficient. For instance, their new REDI program replaces the hard copies associated with purchases with electronic copies that a bookseller can download. Their Harper Tools service allows booksellers to track and keep records about their orders, access their invoices, and even make order corrections — all online.

Simon and Schuster

Website: **www.simonsays.com/content/index.cfm?sid=184**

Simon and Schuster offers a website called Bookseller Resources to help booksellers research and select the books they would like to purchase. The site contains clear links that will give you information about opening a new vendor account, regulations for using co-op money for advertising in your bookstore, their newsletter, catalogs, and more.

AOL Time Warner Book Group

Website: **www.twbookmark.com/catalog/index.shtml**

AOL Time Warner offers an Industry Insiders Booksellers Services page that allows booksellers to download catalogs and other important information. They also feature a section of their site called PubEasy (**www.pubeasy.com/booksellers/book_features.html**), which is the online ordering component of their website aimed directly at booksellers.

The listings above account for only the top five U.S. publishers. There are thousands of publishers all over the world. As you begin to find frontlist books you are interested in, check out who publishes them, contact the publisher, and ask for a book catalog.

You can find publishers through industry resources such as Literary Market Place and Bowker's Books in Print (see the box on the next page). If you join the American Booksellers Association you can obtain a copy of the *ABA Book Buyer's Handbook* which contains information on publishers, including their discounts and payment terms.

Another excellent way to get a number of leads for publishers and wholesalers at one time is to attend one of the many excellent regional or national tradeshow events sponsored by any of the book associations. See more about this in section 2.5.4.

Buying From Wholesalers

Wholesalers, sometimes called distributors or jobbers, buy books from publishers and sell to booksellers.

Just like you must figure out what frontlist and midlist titles you need, you also need to figure out what backlist books to stock for your store. (Backlist books are books that are no longer new releases, but are still very popular with customers and continue to sell well.) You will want to make sure that you stock your shelves with appropriate and successful backlist titles. Here is where wholesalers come in.

First of all, wholesalers buy books from publishers — not just one publisher exclusively, but many of them. So wholesalers can provide a sort of one-stop shop for booksellers to order backlist titles.

As you reorder frontlist titles, you can also check with your wholesaler's rep to see if they have the particular frontlist books you are reordering. This can save you on freight costs (the bookstore is usually responsible for paying for shipping) and paperwork because you will have fewer invoices to pay.

Secondly, wholesalers can ship to you quickly. Many wholesalers can promise you book shipments in just a couple of days. (This is usually faster than a publisher can offer.)

The ability to order and receive books very quickly from wholesalers will make it easier for you to fill special orders for customers interested in buying titles you don't have. It will help you retain and increase customer loyalty.

Finding Publishers

Literary Market Place

One of the best ways to get instant access to a wealth of information for booksellers is to check out Information Today, Inc.'s Literary Market Place website at **www.literarymarketplace. com**. The Literary Market Place, known to insiders as the LMP, has spent the last 50 years compiling a wealth of contact information for the book industry. Inside this guide, booksellers will find a definitive listing of publishers (most of which produce at least three books annually), wholesalers, remainder dealers, distributors, and sales reps in both the U.S. and Canada.

There are several ways to gain access to the guide — including a free browse-only capability; a weekly subscription available for $19.95; an annual subscription fee of $399; or a hard copy version that many libraries purchase. Just by registering you can get the street address of any publisher in the LMP. To view all other pertinent information, you will need to subscribe. (One exception is free access to their small press listings.)

There is also an important section for Industry Services, which is arguably the single most definitive guide for the industry. Plan on spending an hour or two reviewing the site. And bookmark it for future use — you will probably use this reference every day.

R.R. Bowker Inc.

R.R. Bowker has been publishing information products for 130 years. Their Books in Print (**www.booksinprint.com/bip**) is the industry's largest web-based bibliographic resource for professionals. It is a comprehensive database of over five million book, audio book, and video titles. However, subscriptions are expensive, beginning at $1,695 for a single user annual subscription.

If $1,695 is beyond your budget, you might want to consider subscribing to some of Bowker's other products. You can get three issues of *Forthcoming Books* and three issues of *The Bowker Buyer's Guide* for a $299 annual subscription. You can find out more at **www.bowker.com/catalog/000045.htm**.

Some wholesalers will send you a downloadable file of your first purchase that makes the process of adding this information to your own inventory software far easier. Some of the largest wholesalers also stock books on tape and CDs. This makes it easy to purchase these items from them at the same time you place your book inventory order.

Information about major wholesalers is included below. A good starting point for locating smaller wholesalers is the American Wholesale Booksellers Association member list, posted online at **www.awba.com/ wholesaler_members.html**.

After you have checked out the websites of various book wholesalers and decided which ones you would like to work with, you must go through their application process. Naturally, you will have to provide credit references to establish yourself as a bookseller who pays your bills on time.

Baker and Taylor

Website: **www.btol.com/retail.cfm**

Baker and Taylor is one of the major players in the national book wholesaler scene. Their website has a section devoted to helping the book retailer. They sell hardcover, trade paperbacks, children and young adult titles, and audio books.

Additionally, they feature a service called E-Lists (**www.btol.com/elist access.cfm**), which includes lists of available titles grouped by categories designed to save retail booksellers a lot of time. Along with their online ordering feature, this function makes the bookseller's task of shopping for books a lot easier.

Koen Book Distributors

Website: **www.koen.com**

Koen Book Distributors calls itsellf a "full service book wholesaler." Koen's website reads like a book industry newsletter with lots of information and articles about hot books. It also has a number of links to specific features, including areas like "Hot Picks," "Koen Kids," "Independent Press," and more. Some interesting areas include autographed books and the ability to sign up for their free email newsletter. You can order online after they accept your completed application.

Ingram Book Group

Website: **www.ingrambook.com/new/booksellers.asp**

Ingram Book Group is an excellent place for new booksellers to start. The site is extremely easy to navigate, with clear links about how to get started as a new bookseller placing an order for the first time with Ingram.

The site also features information about ipage, a software tool that they have developed especially for booksellers that lets you search for titles, helps you make and track orders, and gives you access to research information like reviews, best-seller lists, and more. You can find out more at **www.ingrambook.com/programs/ipage/default.asp**.

Also check out Ingram Periodicals (**www.ingramperiodicals.com**) to purchase magazines for your bookstore.

4.5.2 Buying Remainder Books

Everyone loves to get a deal! Buying from remainder houses will allow you to get great deals on what are called "overstock" or "hurt books." Many booksellers find that they can get some really interesting, attractive, and low-priced books by ordering from remainder book houses.

The discount you get on remainder books will increase the profit you make. Because your cost is lower, you will achieve a better markup when you sell them in your store. Some wholesalers and publishers will sell you remainder books directly, so it pays to ask. However, here are two book remainder companies to help you start your search:

The Book Depot

Website: **www.allbooksforless.com**

The folks at the The Book Depot call themselves "one of the largest closeout/remainder bookstores in North America." They note on their website that their site is an easy way for booksellers to shop online for remainders. They discount books up to 50 percent and they add an additional 20 percent if the book has some small cosmetic damage (in other words, the book is "hurt").

Chicago International Remainder and Overstock Book Expo

Website: **www.cirobe.com**

This organization holds an annual national tradeshow that is the place for booksellers hoping to learn more about remainders and overstock books and buy them for their stores. Their website is also chock-full of all sorts of insider information about the "bargain book industry." This site is a must-read for all booksellers wanting to learn more about the cost-effective world of remainder books.

4.5.3 Buying Used Books

"The Internet eliminated a lot of the physical work of selling used and rare books, and now it's done electronically, which saves time. What used to be a six-week sale can be over in just a few days. As soon as a book is posted for sale, it is out there for the whole world to buy, and it can sell in just a few hours."

— Al Navis, Almark and Company Booksellers
Toronto, Ontario

If you are unfamiliar with how booksellers buy used books, you will be amazed at how different it is from buying new books. In used book sales there is a wide variety of ways to get inventory.

Book Fairs

As a used bookstore owner, you might buy from church, city, or nonprofit organization-sponsored book fairs. Many booksellers travel around the country to buy books at various book fairs. Sometimes a book fair will be right in your own city or in one nearby.

At these book fairs, books are greatly discounted. For example, in the case of book fairs like the Volunteer Nonprofit Service Association (VNSA) in Phoenix, Arizona, most books are sold for one dollar or less and, on the last day of the sale, every book (with the exception of rare books) is sold for half off the marked price. It is normal to get lovely hardcover books for fifty cents each on the last day of the sale. (See the box on the next page for more about the author's experience with this book fair.)

A Fabulous Book Fair

The VNSA book fair is an annual event held during February at the county fairgrounds in Phoenix, Arizona. After paying for parking, you walk into the fair and pick up a map that shows you how the categories of books are arranged inside. Shopping carts and boxes are provided if you would like to use them. The categories are well-marked and easy to see. As you stroll along the long tables of books inside the fair, you will see rows and rows of books of all descriptions.

If it is early in the sale, there will still be many boxes of books underneath the tables. As soon as room becomes available, these books are transferred to the tables. At the beginning of the fair you have the best chance to pick up modern first editions and other valuable books. On the last day of the event the books are half price, except for the selection of rare books, and there are many bargains. Knowing what you are looking for ahead of time is half the battle.

I walked away with $27.50 worth of books — over 60 titles! I found a modern first edition of a Jack Smith book called *Alive in La La Land* in excellent condition with a dust jacket. A used book resale site called Abebooks.com lists this title in a similar condition for $27.50. So in essence, if I sell my modern first edition, all the other books I purchased were really free. As a bookseller, you can see that if you know how to hunt, it's possible to pay for a whole day of book buying with one lucky find.

The staff at this event was friendly and informed, and the method of getting from the event floor through the purchase line was highly organized. As pay stations became available, volunteers waved signs to get people to walk to the next place to pay. Finally, I showed my receipt upon leaving and walked my heavy purchase over to a tent area in its original shopping cart. The volunteer gave me a ticket to claim it and I drove my car directly up to the tent. All in all, it was an extremely well planned, enjoyable event — and I even got a modern first edition!

You can find out more about the VNSA book fair at its website, **www.vnsabooksale.org**.

One excellent way to be aware of book fairs that happen around the country is a website called Book Sale Finder, which allows you to sign up for email alerts about book sales anywhere in the U.S. and Canada. You can customize the alerts based on the number of miles you are willing to travel from your home to attend book sales, fairs, auctions, and other used book events. With their regular email notification, you will be aware of up-and-coming used book sales in your area.

If you sell old and rare books, the site also posts classified ads for those who are looking for specific books. For ten dollars a month, this is an excellent way to advertise books you are interested in, too. Visit Book Sale Finder at **www.book-sales-in-america.com**.

Buying From Your Customers

When you open your doors you will have another avenue to find used books — your own customers. Buying books from customers will help you to continuously add to your store's inventory, but it will not help you with your opening inventory — the customers come after the store is open.

However, Lori Soard, author of the *FabJob Guide to Become a Second-hand Store Owner*, advises: "Do not worry about having the store full before you open. You will be surprised at how quickly the inventory will come in."

Think about how you will pay customers for the books they bring in and how you will determine which books you want. Some booksellers buy books outright, some take them on consignment (discussed below), while others allow customers to trade books. You will have to decide what works best for you.

For example, you might have a policy of paying sellers a flat fee of 25% of the book's original retail price (which you could then mark up and resell for 50% of the retail price). To encourage customers who supply your books to take books in trade, you might offer 40% of the price you sell it for (or 20% of the original retail price) if the customer opts for cash and 50% of the selling price (25% of the original retail price) if they opt for trade.

Consignment

Consignment stores take in items from customers and sell them for a percentage of the profits. A typical split is 60/40, with 60 percent of the sale price going to the store to cover overhead expenses and generate a profit and 40 percent going to the consignee who has left their books with you.

Consignment can be an inexpensive way to build inventory, because you do not have to pay for the product until it has sold. You can stock your store with merchandise without paying it up front.

Resale

The main difference between a consignment store and a resale store is that resale stores typically buy used items outright and resell them.

Often, you will have more of an investment upfront, but if you find a good deal and are able to resell for a substantial profit, then you keep all the profit and do not have to split it with a client. Resale store owners often pick up items at auctions, garage sales, or buy them outright from customers.

To decide what to do with your own store, visit a number of local used bookstores and ask what their policy is for purchasing books from customers. Chances are, you will find different stores have different policies. For example, many stores will only purchase recent titles of books in certain genres (i.e. business books published within the past three years or travel guides published within the past five years).

> **TIP:** You can find out how old books are by checking the copyright date printed within the first few pages of a book.

Online

While online booksellers will usually charge more than other sources, you can sometimes find great deals online. For example, Tartan Book Sales is a company that specializes in reselling books that have been circulated through libraries. They will remove the library cards and clean the books for you for an additional fee. You can find out more about their services at **www.tartanbooks.com/bulkbooks.htm**.

Other Ideas

Here are some of the many other ways to get inventory for your bookstore. Chances are you won't need to use these ideas after you open your store, but they can certainly help you get your starting inventory:

- Yard sales – you can save even more by bartering on the price

- Goodwill

- Book sales sponsored by local schools, colleges, universities and libraries

- Estate sales

- Run a classified ad in the local newspaper offering to buy used books

- Send announcements to friends and post notices on community bulletin boards

4.5.4 Deciding What Books to Buy

"Being the buyer is one of the biggest tasks of a bookstore owner. It requires going through catalogs and determining what you are going to buy. It's a very fun job, and at the same time, there is a very large level of seriousness in it. You need a very strong sense of what your budget is so you know exactly what you are going to spend for each section of your store in any new season, and how much you are going to spend with each vendor."

— Mary Ellen Kavanaugh, My Sisters' Words
Syracuse, New York

With tens of thousands of books to choose from, how do you decide which books to buy for your store? Three factors to consider are:

- Your categories

- Your budget

- What you think will sell

Categories

The categories you decide to carry in your bookstore will help you narrow down your choices. If you choose a specific market niche, you will have fewer categories than another bookseller who sells books for a more generalized audience. A list of categories is provided in section 2.3.2 of this guide.

Sales reps from wholesalers can be very helpful in the process of determining your beginning categories. Most wholesalers' sales reps have worked with independent booksellers in all specialty areas and it is their business to help you figure out what to order.

Another way to get ideas about the best categories for your bookstore is to check out the competition. Go to bookstores in your area and see how they have organized their categories.

As in the case of Mary Gay Shipley, owner of That Bookstore in Blytheville, Arkansas, your categories may change based on the preferences or requests of your customers. At one point in the early days of her store, Shipley's teenage customers requested that she carry science fiction and fantasy. Up until this request from teenagers in her community, this was not a category that she had considered for her store. But she listened to her customers and made buying decisions that increased her customer base.

Your categories, and the amount of books you have in each one, will be based in part on your budget for books. As you determine your categories, you will have some that are definite musts, and some that would be nice if you can manage it.

Your Budget

Your inventory budget will depend upon how much money you have, how much space you have for books, and whether you are opening a new, used, or combination bookstore. In most cases, your inventory of books will be your most expensive start-up cost.

In the American Booksellers Association booklet *Opening a Bookstore — An Introduction to Retail Bookselling*, author Donna Paz Kaufman mentions an example case for consideration when buying inventory.

Kaufman suggests that if a typical bookseller has an average cost of $10 per book, and has $80,000 dollars to invest for book inventory, they will have to select 8,000 books to fill their store.

Naturally, if you have more money to invest, you will get more books, but as you can see, selecting inventory for your store will probably be the largest and most important task you must complete before you can open your bookstore.

According to the American Booksellers Association's *Manual on Bookselling: Practical Advice for the Bookstore Professional*, an out of print publication edited by Kate Whouley with Linda Miller and Rosemary Hawkins:

> "The dollars you allot to initial store inventory depend on the figures you have projected for sales. If you project a sales volume of $150,000 and anticipate an inventory turn (the total sales per year divided by the average inventory at retail) of three, your start-up inventory should be $50,000 at retail."

Publishers set a retail price for each book they publish. However, the actual amount a bookseller retails the book for may vary from the publisher's suggested retail price.

For example, Amazon.com sells a number of titles for less than the publisher's retail price. Of course, in order to make a profit, booksellers buy the books for less than the retail price.

The resources listed above for finding publishers have information about the discounts they offer and their terms of payment. Typical terms are:

- A discount of 40% is average (so an inventory worth $50,000 at retail would cost you $30,000).

- The more books you buy, the higher the discount.

- Discounts on non-trade titles such as textbooks may be only 20%.

- The bookstore usually pays the freight (the cost to ship the books from the publisher to the bookstore).

- If you have good credit you may be able to wait 30 days or more to pay for the books.

- If books don't sell you can return them for other books.

TIP: When wholesalers sell you what they call an "opening store inventory," in many cases you will be able to return books to them during the first year with minimum trouble and penalty. Although unlikely to be necessary, you can also get a refund for your inventory. Make sure to check the policy of any wholesaler ahead of time.

What You Think Will Sell

Learning which books are likely to sell is an ongoing process. A variety of research sources are available (as are a number of professionals in both selling and consulting capacities) to help you. But before you contact anyone, you need to think about the books you like and want for your store.

TIP: If you don't have any idea where to start, begin your research with the books you are really excited about — those books you truly love.

You will research the books you want to buy for your store every day you are in business. Getting information is key in knowing what books to buy. Consider these resources as an excellent start for research:

- Industry publications

- Regional and national bookselling association websites

- Your local newspaper

- Tradeshows

- Publisher's catalogs

- The movie and arts listings of your local paper

- Other booksellers

- Wholesaler's databases and suggestions for beginning book inventories

- Your family and friends

- Your neighborhood librarian (don't forget to talk to a children's librarian if you are planning on stocking children's titles)

Basic Buying Tips

Even if you have never been a professional "buyer," you have certainly bought things in your life. Many of the same principles prudent shoppers use in any buying situation prevail when buying for your own bookstore.

Before you begin to buy for your store, you need to figure out what to buy, how much to spend, and how to be a savvy buyer. When beginning to buy for your bookstore, remember to consider these things:

- Find other bookstores you like, and see what they sell.

- Decide what you want and what helps you define your store's niche.

- Take advice, but trust your own research and instincts.

- Find out where to get what you want.

- Comparison shop before you buy.

- Contact potential vendors and get the facts.

- Find out terms.

- Find out how to buy.

- Negotiate if possible.

Book reviews can get customers into your bookstore asking about a new book. So it's a good idea to keep up with reviews in industry publications such as *Publisher's Weekly*. (See chapter 7 of this guide for industry publications.)

> *"I think it is just as important to read the publications that tell you about the books as it is to read the books. But it's important to remember that a review is just one person's opinion. There have been many times I haven't agreed with what the New York Times has said about a book."*
>
> — John Brancati, East End Books
> East Hampton, New York

Also check industry sources such as those mentioned elsewhere in this guide. For example, the following is excellent advice from an American Library Association pamphlet written by the late Peter Van Wingen, Specialist for the Book Arts, Rare and Special Collections Division at the Library of Congress:

> "The age of a book has very little to do with its value. Dealers, collectors, and librarians, however, do use some broad time spans to establish dates of likely importance: e.g., all books printed before 1501, English books printed before 1641, books printed in the Americas before 1801 and books printed west of the Mississippi before 1850. These dates are rough guidelines at best and are always subject to the overriding factors of intrinsic importance, condition, and demand."

More information from this pamphlet can be found at **www.rbms. nd.edu/ yob.html**.

In addition, check out the top sellers lists at superstores like Amazon.com and Barnes and Noble, as well as book reviews in large national newspapers like USA Today and the New York Times.

- *USA Today's Top 150 Best-Selling Books List*
  www.usatoday.com/life/books/top-50.htm

- *The New York Times Best-Seller Lists*
  www.nytimes.com/pages/books/bestseller

4.5.5 Buying Sidelines

Customers buying books also like to buy other things. If you sell those things, you will make more sales. In a typical visit to a superstore, you might see several large shelves devoted entirely to sidelines. As an exercise, I traveled to a bookstore and spent five minutes writing down every sideline I could see. Here is just a brief list of sidelines that I could count in less than five minutes:

- Mugs

- Notebooks

- Journals

- Toys

- Makeup

- Small gifts — many related to holiday themes

- Festively packaged food appropriate for holidays — like boxes of beautiful Valentine's candy

- Kitchen tools to be sold with cookbooks

- Jewelry

- Mouse pads

- Notes cards

- Greeting cards

- Stationery

- Decorative home items

- Wind chimes

- Playing cards

- Jokes and magic tricks

- Candy

- Bookmarks

- Gift bags

- Tiny reading lights for reading in bed

- Earphones for playing books on tape

- Small stuffed toys

Imagine how you can create lovely displays by combining books and various related gifts. Think about how people buying presents and gifts will remember that your store carries everything they need to get in and out with a great complete gift, including the gift bag and the greeting card.

Where to Order Sidelines

If you see sidelines you like in the bookstores you visit, first write down the name of the manufacturer and any other pertinent information you can find and do a web search. You may be able to find the manufacturer's company online instantly.

Just like the book industry uses tradeshows to sell products, so does the gift industry. Many craft, toy, and other gift manufacturers attend national gift fairs and tradeshows and this is an excellent place to meet face-to-face with the people who you want to choose as vendors for your bookstore. GreatRep.com has a list of trade shows that are happening around the world at **www.greatrep.com/trade_shows.asp**.

Using Local Talent

Some bookstores use an eclectic mix of sideline manufacturers and providers including local artists and jewelry makers. Consider letting artists and jewelry makers sell their products in your bookstore on consignment. This is one way to make a small profit on what they sell without paying upfront for the products themselves. Make sure you are clear about your expectations and put your agreement in writing.

4.5.6 Setting Your Prices

There are two important issues that you must consider when setting your prices for books and other merchandise in your bookstore — cost and price. Cost is the total amount it costs you to sell anything in your store. Price is the amount you charge your customer. And remember the formula:

$$Price - Cost = Profit\ (or\ Loss)$$

Know the Basics

Here's a very brief look at some basics you need to understand in order to see how your cost and your price relate to your ability to make a profit:

- Direct costs, or variable costs, are costs associated with the product itself.

- Fixed costs are those costs that remain the same. (These are sometimes called overhead costs.)

- Direct costs plus fixed costs equals the cost of goods sold (how much it costs you to sell your product).

- Gross profit is the selling price you charge minus direct costs.

- Net profit is gross profit minus fixed costs.

- The breakeven point is the place where your income from sales equals your total costs. Selling more than your breakeven point creates a profit. Selling less creates a loss.

So here is the goal: Sell enough merchandise at a price that will cover your total costs and make a profit. But you must remember to charge only what your customers are willing to pay... charging more than the publisher's retail list price or less than your own purchase price would be foolish.

Price your books to be competitive, but don't price yourself out of business. Your book prices should both attract customers and help you maintain a healthy profit margin.

Increasing Your Profit Margin

When ordering new books, you can increase your profit margin by purchasing at a higher discount rate. One way to do this is to buy from publishers rather than wholesalers or distributors; publishers often send books free of shipping charges.

You can also get higher discounts by purchasing hurt books and remainders, or backlist or midlist titles, which are less expensive than frontlist titles. Watch for other opportunities, such as purchasing in quantities that offer high discounts. If 1 to 49 copies have a 40 percent discount, 50 to 99 may have a 50 percent discount. In some cases, these quantities must be all the same title, but in others you may purchase mixed titles and acquire a larger selection of books.

Don't forget that bookseller tradeshows offer special discounts — another good reason to join your booksellers association and participate in these events.

Pricing Sidelines

The price you charge for your sidelines is up to you. You must remember to price sidelines to cover your cost, make a profit, and sell based on what your customers will pay. If you want to sell ballpoint pens for one hundred dollars each, you won't sell any. You might not even be able to sell them for one dollar. You must determine what the market will bear.

Pricing Used Books

Just as you can choose your own system of payment for buying used books, you can choose your own system of pricing. One option is to charge a percentage of the retail price. So if a book sold new for $9.95, you would offer the seller $2.49 and then resell it for $4.98. If a book doesn't sell at that price by a particular time, you could cut the price further.

An excellent tool that booksellers in the used and rare book industry swear by is Abebooks (**www.abebooks.com**). This giant database of books allows you to sell books online and gather information about books you want to find. By searching for a specific book in the database, you can quickly see what the market will bear for a specific title.

I picked up a book at the VNSA book sale called *The Royal Road to Romance*, by Richard Halliburton. I was previously unfamiliar with this book, so just for kicks I checked the market on Abebooks.com. I was amazed and gratified to find that several copies of the same edition, in the same condition, were going for about $50. I paid fifty cents for it. I have a potential 10,000 percent profit margin if I can sell this book to an interested collector.

Competition and Price

Can you compete with large book superstores? No. Superstores sell more volume at higher customer discounts than you can afford as an independent bookseller. So what you must do is look for creative ways to increase profits in other areas. Remember, as an independent bookseller you sell more than just books and sidelines. You sell personal service, expert knowledge, and atmosphere — all things that make people want to buy at independent bookstores. This is how you get your competitive edge.

As a future bookstore owner, you will be happy to learn that several trends suggest that a surge of interest in smaller, independent bookstores, including used bookstores, is underway. These trends have been noted by *Newsweek* and by *Inc.com* in a feature on small businesses centered on the theme "small is big again."

Independent bookstores have unique qualities their owners can use in competing with large book superstores. For example, as an independent bookseller you can

- Sell sidelines from local suppliers on a consignment or commission basis.

- Hold receptions for local artists and display their art for purchase.

- Promote "one of a kind" book titles rather than large quantities of one book title.

- Barter with other businesses; place a small lending library in a nearby café or hotel lobby.

- Create a small space for book club discussions and lectures.

- Hold story times for children, especially during the holidays.

- Set a mood with music to tantalize your customers (classical music, Celtic songs, café music from Paris, etc.).

4.5.7 Controlling Your Inventory

Inventory that sits on the shelf takes cash out of your business. As a standard, the average turnover for a healthy inventory is three times a year. To control your inventory, and make sure turnover is healthy, you will want to track your sales within each category over a specified time frame and then compare them with sales from the previous time frame.

This will tell you what's moving and what's not, and when sales are occurring within certain categories. You may discover variations by month or season, and you will be able to compare your figures with industry and geographical averages, and eventually your sales from previous years.

On the basis of your tracking and comparisons, create a schedule for reordering books and sidelines, setting realistic and affordable targets. With an average turnover of inventory three times a year, a bookseller can plan and budget for orders approximately every four months.

Plan to have books arrive to coincide with seasonal interests and needs, and order them far in advance to save on shipping fees. Shipping is higher when merchandise is needed in a hurry. The least expensive shipping for books is via "media mail," which has a shipping time of two to four weeks.

Inventory that is slow moving should be reduced for quick sale or returned, if possible. Publishers and wholesalers have varying policies on the return of books previously sold to booksellers. When books are initially purchased, the bookseller has discount options that favor buying on a "non-returnable" basis. This averages at a 50 percent discount. When a bookseller purchases on a "returnable" basis, the discount is lower, generally about 40 percent. Unsold books may occasionally be returned for credit against future purchases.

Preventing Theft

A final word about inventory: Be certain to protect against loss. Sometimes books walk out the door. An independent bookseller may not even be aware this is occurring unless inventory is accounted for very closely. When inventory control is haphazard, it's a lot more difficult to catch and deal with inventory loss.

A simple preventative measure, besides maintaining a tight inventory control system, is to acknowledge your customers in a personal manner when they come into your store. If they have backpacks, you might suggest a spot where they can "lighten their load."

Developing a rapport with your customers will make theft less likely, as it's easier to take something that's not your own when it represents a mere object rather than the property of a person you know.

You might have to install security measures such as mirrors, cameras, or an alarm system. Asking a security specialist to discuss loss prevention measures with you and your employees is good business, and may decrease your insurance rates as well.

5. Store Operations

5.1 Establishing Procedures

5.1.1 Developing an Operations Manual

As you move through the process of opening your bookstore, you will begin to notice that you are starting to develop routines about how you do things. These routines will eventually fall under the more official business term — operations.

One of the great things about owning your bookstore is that you are in charge of deciding the routine, or your operations, and you can plan how things run in your bookstore to satisfy your needs and desires.

Every time you do something, keep a record of how you did it. As you go along, take accurate notes about what works, what doesn't work, and what will need to be done a different way.

Over time you will begin to see an organized system emerge — this is the beginning of developing your operational procedures. Consider the following questions:

- What did I accomplish?

- What business or individual did I contact?

- What was the contact's name, address, phone number, and email?

- What steps did I take to complete this task?

- Was this method successful?

- What should be changed?

Once you record your answers for the questions above, you will have the basics for putting together a written record of your store's methods and procedures for your employees.

This way, no matter where you are, your store will run the way you want it to. You can't always be in your bookstore, and eventually there will come a day where you leave the responsibility of your store to one of your qualified and responsible employees.

Bookstore procedures aren't necessarily things that you can store in your head. Having written records and instructions of important store procedures and tasks makes it possible for you to help your bookstore employees complete tasks themselves.

For instance, it is hard to remember all the passwords and codes for things, the procedures for receiving a shipment of books, or the steps in taking a check from a customer. The best thing to do is to make a guide for employees (and for you) to keep this information organized and accessible.

Making an operations manual for your bookstore will help you get all of your procedures and instructions for every little task organized and in one spot for you and your employees to refer to. Follow the simple directions on the next page to make your own Bookstore Operations Manual.

What You Need

Here are the things you'll need to create your manual:

❑ Checklists for each area of the store (more on this in a minute)

❑ Three-ring binder or folder with clear plastic insert space on cover and spine

❑ Three-hole punch

❑ Binder dividers with section labels

❑ Checklist forms

❑ Task forms

❑ Special reminder forms

❑ Emergency forms

What to Do

Once you have gathered your materials, follow these steps:

• Carefully consider each area of your operations. Make binder divider tags with the following labels: Opening Tasks, Closing Tasks, Daily Tasks, Weekly Tasks, Monthly Tasks, Quarterly Tasks, Annual Tasks. Place these labeled dividers in the binder.

• Make a checklist for each area. List the tasks that you can think of for each area. Remember to write down important reminder information like where things are located, which lights to turn on, etc. Think about how you would instruct someone unfamiliar with the task to do it. Sequentially ordered steps work best.

- Fill out a separate sequential form or reminder sheet for each specific area of operations in your store.

- Make a list of emergency numbers and other emergency information for the first page of the binder. You might want to place a copy of every employee's emergency information card inside the binder directly behind the emergency number and procedure page.

- Label the binder clearly and make a copy of all the contents to store in a safe place away from your bookstore.

TIP: Remember that this operations manual will be fluid and change over time. As you change your procedures, remember to change the corresponding task page.

Here are some examples of various areas of the store and some things in each area that you might want to include in your operations manual:

Areas of Operations Checklists

Opening/Closing

❑ Door locks

❑ Lights — both indoor and outdoor

❑ Security systems and codes

❑ What to do if the alarm goes off accidentally

❑ Turning on/off the air-conditioning and heating units

❑ Turning on/off computers/fax/postal machine/copier

❑ Checking the sidewalk and front entrance

❑ Mail sorting and opening

❑ Brewing coffee

- ❏ Email

- ❏ Answering machine

- ❏ Cleaning break room staff kitchen area

Cash Wrap

- ❏ Operating the cash register

- ❏ Preparing money drawer for opening

- ❏ Processing credit and debit cards

- ❏ Processing checks

- ❏ Accepting and selling gift certificates

- ❏ Enrolling customers in book buyers' club

- ❏ Completing a transaction

- ❏ Keeping track of what is sold/Inventory

- ❏ Phone procedures

- ❏ Directions to store

- ❏ Giving information about special store events

- ❏ Using computers/fax/postal machine/copier

- ❏ Looking up books

- ❏ Mailing list

- ❏ Promotions and sales

- ❏ Cash deposits and bank deposits

- ❏ Wrapping gifts

Floor Procedures

- ❏ Shelving new books and returning books into order
- ❏ Cleaning and organizing displays
- ❏ Making new displays
- ❏ Sale displays
- ❏ Holiday displays

Customer Service

- ❏ Answering questions
- ❏ Looking up books
- ❏ Ordering special orders for customers

Receiving Shipments/Warehouse/Stockroom

- ❏ Procedures for receiving shipments
- ❏ Procedures for shipping to another location
- ❏ Shipping contacts
- ❏ Procedures for moving stock to the floor

Inventory/Ordering/Purchasing

- ❏ Logging purchased books
- ❏ Vendor lists and contacts
- ❏ Purchase orders
- ❏ Ordering procedures
- ❏ Credit references

Safety/Health/Emergency Procedures

- ❑ Emergency contact numbers — fire, police, hospitals, etc.

- ❑ Staff and owner emergency contact numbers

- ❑ Procedures for emergency in-store illness — for both staff members and customers

- ❑ Evacuation procedures

- ❑ Terrorism or natural disaster plan

- ❑ What to do in case of shoplifting

- ❑ What to do in case of robbery

5.1.2 Your Employee Handbook

An employee handbook allows you to put into writing all the rules and practices that you want your bookstore staff to follow. It also gives you a written document that employees read and sign, stating that they understand your bookstore policies and rules and agree to follow them.

This is an important security precaution that helps you to protect yourself and your store from liability issues. Written policies make clear ahead of time what employees are expected to do and how they are expected to behave at work.

You don't have to be a writer to make your own employee handbook. Even if you don't create a complete employee handbook, you should still have employees read and sign a rules and procedures document.

Creating Rules and Procedures

The best way to start is to plan out your own employee agreement. Use the suggestions on the next few pages to make a list of all the things that you want to include in your rules and procedures document.

Attendance

Before you decide on your attendance rules and policies, consider these questions:

- What shifts will bookstore employees work?

- Will they be required to come to work a few minutes early?

- Will they keep a time card, or will you have a time clock?

- Will you have different procedures for café employees, or will they log their hours the same way bookstore employees do?

- Will you allow them to switch shifts with other employees?

- Will you accommodate school or personal schedules? How will employees notify you about changes in their personal schedules?

- Will you arrange time off for jury duty or for bereavement or emergency leave?

Paying Employees

Before you decide on your pay rules and policies, consider these questions:

- How often will bookstore employees be paid?

- Will you arrange overtime hours?

- How often will they be reviewed for performance and/or receive raises?

- Will you offer employees direct deposit?

- Will you have a commission structure? How will employees be paid their commission earnings?

- What will your policies be about vacation pay?

- What will your policies and rules be about benefits if you decide to offer them?

Employee Standards of Behavior

Before you decide on your standards of behavior rules and policies, consider these questions:

- How will you state rules and policies about drugs, alcohol, and weapons in the workplace?

- How will you state your sexual harassment policies?

- How will you state policies about violence or abusiveness in the workplace to fellow employees or customers?

- Will you have a dress code or rules about acceptable appearance?

- Will you mention rules about attitude, standards of courtesy, or customer service?

Safety Rules and Procedures

Before you decide on your safety rules and procedures, consider these questions:

- Will you require that employees fill out emergency contact forms?

- What rules will you have regarding medical emergencies?

- Will you give employees an evacuation plan?

- What will you expect employees to do in a national emergency?

- What will you expect employees to do in a natural emergency such as earthquake, fire, flood, or tornado?

- Where will you keep your first aid kit? Will all employees have access to it?

- If someone gets hurt, what reporting procedures will you use?

General Employee Rules

Before you decide on your general employee rules and policies, consider these questions:

- Will you have a break room or a designated place for employees to eat lunch?

- Will you offer employees a refrigerator, microwave and coffee? What will the rules be regarding these appliances?

- Will employees be able to buy food from the café? At a discount?

- Will you offer book discounts to employees? To their families?

- What will your smoking policy be?

- What will your rules be regarding breaks?

- Will you require any employee training or outside classes or seminars for your staff?

5.2 Technology

Technology is a bookstore owner's best friend. Most booksellers interviewed for this book feel that technology has singlehandedly changed the way they have done business over the last ten years. In many cases they feel it has made what they do dramatically easier.

Wise booksellers know that the Internet and changes in technology are helpful to the book industry. Booksellers have their inventories on computer. They do their payroll, accounting and taxes on computer. They read about new books and stay connected to the various bookselling associations to which they belong online.

To make your bookstore the very best it can be and keep up with the book industry on a global level, you must be ready to use technology in your bookstore. But don't worry; you don't have to be a computer genius or a computer nerd to make computers work for you. With a little practice and a little help, even the most novice users can have the benefits of technology working for them!

"We have six computers and I don't know how we could live without them. I dedicated one entire bookseller's convention to investigating the kind of software I wanted to buy. I found the software I wanted, and a sales rep showed me what to do."

— Mary Gay Shipley, That Bookstore in Blytheville
Blytheville, Arkansas

5.2.1 Your Computer System

Having the proper computer equipment and software can really help any businessperson to be successful. If you think about what you hope to accomplish with technology in your store, you will be able to determine the sort of system you want with all the bells and whistles.

Before you run out and start buying computers and software, consider the tasks you would like to accomplish with the computers in your bookstore. Some of the things you might want to use your computer system for include:

- Managing your entire inventory of books

- Managing your inventory of sidelines

- Keeping your bookstore's records

- Researching books on the Internet

- Ordering online

- Creating your newsletter

- Sending your email newsletter

- Paying your bills

- Looking up books in your inventory for customers

- Making and printing flyers, cards, stationery, and other business forms

- Making invitations

- Doing your payroll

- Organizing your taxes

The Hardware

In addition to a basic computer system, you will need:

- Scanner

- Printer

- Recordable CD drive

- Extension cords

- Surge strips

The Software

There are hundreds of good software choices for small businesses, and there are specific programs designed for booksellers. (See section 5.2.2 for more details.) As you go along, you will learn more and more about the software you need for your particular bookstore. But for now, the "musts" include:

- Office suite software, including publishing software and a word processing program

- An inventory program designed for the bookselling industry

- Net browsing software so you can surf the net

- Anti-virus and firewall software to protect your computer and files

- Web design software, if you decide to create and maintain your own website

- Accounting software to help you balance your books and pay your bills and employees

Again, as with hardware, expert knowledge is vital. Research what you want carefully and become as informed as you can before you invest in your technology equipment.

Networking

If you have a number of computers in your bookstore and you want them to all work together, they will have to be networked. If you do not have a lot of experience setting up a small business computer network, now is the time to get help. There will be many computer consultants in your local area who specialize in helping small businesses with their needs. Doing thorough research before you commit to a computer system is vital in making your bookstore a technological success.

Besides connecting the computers in your store to each other, you will also want to consider connecting them to the outside world — the Internet. Getting the very best Internet connection you can will save you years of wasted time, frustration, and heartache.

Just a few years ago, the only way you could access the Internet was through what was called "dial-up." Now the only people who use dial-up are occasional home users. Most businesses do not use dial-up — it is simply too slow. You will want to invest in either DSL or cable modem connections.

To find out what high-speed Internet service is available in your area, visit **www.dslreports.com**. You can search for different types of service based on your ZIP code.

You can now get wireless connection equipment that will allow users with wireless networking cards to connect anywhere in your store without plugging in their computers. Some book superstores have jumped on this idea to give their bookstores an urbane, uptown feel. This great tool will bring smart people with computers into your bookstore and help you attract a sophisticated clientele with money to spend.

5.2.2 Managing Your Inventory

Once you have an inventory of books, you need organize it in a way that will allow you to find the books you have and know when you need to reorder specific titles.

The system you create should allow you to order, reorder, accept returns, and organize with ease. Most booksellers choose to computerize their inventory tasks. Inventory software should allow you to:

- Enter every book in your store into a large database

- See the title, author, and category of each book and where it is placed on your shelves

- Check the cost of each book and the price you are charging for it

- Determine the number of copies of each title you have and remind you when to reorder

- Determine which books have sold and when they sold

- Help you track buying and sales trends

- Run reports to see your daily, weekly, and monthly inventory reports

- Track books by stock number and/or bar code, ISBN number, price, date purchased, and sales price

- Connect your inventory to your sales with a Point of Sale (POS) system

There are a variety of different and excellent software programs developed just for independent and smaller bookstores. Plan on gathering information about a number of them (an excellent place to do so is a tradeshow) before you decide what will work the best for your store and your specific needs. Here are a few examples to get you started:

- *Books In Store*
  www.booksinstore.com

- *Booklog*
  www.booklog.com

- *Bookstore Management Product and Solutions*
  (Offers software created specifically for Christian bookstores)
  www.bsmgr.com/solutions

- *Wordstock*
  www.wordstock.com

5.2.3 Bookkeeping

Keeping your books is a business concept that includes two things:

- How much money you have coming in

- How much money you have going out

It really is simple. Even if you didn't excel in mathematics and you have never taken an accounting class, there are a number of excellent accounting and business software programs available to help you set up your books simply, without doing all the "brain time" yourself.

In addition to the software mentioned above for the bookstore industry, there are a variety of generic bookkeeping programs such as Quicken and Quickbooks. Even though software can make most of the work easier for you, you might consider taking a beginning accounting class at a local community college. Accounting basics are vital information that all booksellers need, but sometimes neglect to learn.

Accounting Methods

Single Entry Accounting

A lot of bookstore owners who have small stores and are just starting out begin with what is called single entry accounting. This sort of accounting is about as basic as the kind you use to pay your everyday household expenses. It requires that you log your revenue – the money you make, and your expenditures – or the money you spend.

Double Entry Accounting

Double entry accounting is a term that all bookkeepers are familiar with. The system was developed over 700 years ago and was originally thought to be a method by which bookkeepers could check their mathematics twice. In double entry accounting, you make two entries for each trans-action — one to show you where the money came from, and another to show you where it goes. With the advent of software that does this for you, the concept isn't quite as vital, but the name remains.

Reports You Should Know About

At the very least, even if you plan on having a full-time bookkeeper or accountant, you should know enough about your bookstore's books to be able to do them yourself if you need to, and certainly to be able to check the accuracy and honesty of those whom you employ.

You should know how to:

- Make a daily sales report of how much money you take in every day

- Make accounts payable and accounts receivable reports

- Make and read an income statement (also called a profit and loss statement)

- Make and read a cash flow statement

- Understand a balance sheet

The Daily Sales Report

Every day you take in money. You get cash, you take credit cards, and possibly debit cards for payment, and you may even accept checks. A daily sales report logs all of this information. It will also help you ready the monies you take in for your bank deposit. Most accounting software will allow you to enter this information. Some booksellers do this by hand — they create or buy a form to use and put the daily proceeds in an envelope. You will want to check your cash register receipts against what you actually have in your cash drawer to make sure it all matches at the end of each day.

Accounts Payable and Accounts Receivable Reports

Accounts payable are those accounts that you must pay — the money or bills your bookstore owes. Accounts receivable are those accounts that are owed your bookstore — the money that others owe you.

Accounts payable reports will tell you what bills you owe and when they are due. It's important to know clearly what you owe before you make any additional purchases. You have to be able to pay all your incoming bills and still have enough money for the other things you need to purchase for your business. An accounts payable report will help you to schedule when you will pay your bills, and will help you make sure nothing is neglected or forgotten.

Accounts receivable reports will vary widely depending on how you do business. For instance, accepting credit cards or selling books over the Internet will affect how this report looks.

Income Statement (Profit and Loss Statement)

Your income statement (also called a profit and loss statement) will tell you how much money you have in expenses and how much money you have in revenue. A number of things are necessary for an income statement. You need to know:

- *Your sales* — Your gross sales minus returns and your discounts

- *The cost of goods sold* — The cost of your goods and what it costs you to sell them in your bookstore

- *Your gross profit* — Subtract your cost of goods from your sales

- *Your operating expenses* — Everything you must pay for to operate your bookstore, including depreciation

- *Your net profit before and after taxes* — Subtract your operating expenses from your gross profit, and then subtract your tax liability

The end result will tell you how much money your bookstore is making — what is commonly referred to as the "bottom line."

Cash Flow Statement

Cash flow is an important element of your financial picture. With a cash flow statement you will be able to see where the cash is in your business and how you are paying for things. It lets you look at how your business is making it from day to day. Are you paying expenses with the money you take in from your operating expenses, or are you paying for expenses with other business funds? If you are doing so with the former, your business is self-sustaining.

The term cash flow is really an accurate term — cash coming in and going out of your business. Cash flow statements concern the net cash flowing in and out of your bookstore through operating, investing, and financing activities.

Balance Sheet

A good metaphor for a balance sheet would be if you could get a camera and take an aerial view photo of your bookstore's financial situation. A balance sheet is the quickest way to see how your bookstore is doing at a glance. Think of it this way: It shows you what you own and what you owe. In other words, it is a balance of your assets and your liabilities.

Here are some of the terms to become familiar with when preparing or reading your bookstore's balance sheet:

- Assets (both fixed and current)

- Liabilities (both current and long-term)

- Owner's equity

One thing to remember about a balance sheet is that it is a snapshot and the information compiled may change daily.

5.3 Employees

One of the most challenging aspects of running your own bookstore is finding knowledgeable, friendly, reliable, honest employees to work in it!

Great employees can help any business succeed. They can represent your store and build their own loyal customers. They can make your bookstore a place where people want to go because they know that they will be treated with friendliness and respect. Great employees have ideas to make your store better. At their best, they become people you trust your store to when you are somewhere else. They protect your interests and they help you make a profit.

Many bookstore owners feel like they have set themselves up to be the only person who customers feel comfortable coming to with questions, or for advice. While it is flattering to be all things to all people, the reality of the situation is that you need staff members to whom you can trust your store during those times when you are not there. In order to operate effectively, you need someone who can handle the store while you are out attending association meetings, traveling to tradeshows, or even just going to lunch.

To determine who you want to work in your bookstore, you must decide what sort of professional qualifications, attitudes, and work ethic you are looking for. This is a vital step in actually finding the right employees. Getting a clear understanding of who you want to work in your store will help you figure out how to go about getting that sort of person.

5.3.1 Qualities of Great Bookstore Employees

Have you ever gone into a bookstore and been treated rudely or without concern by an employee?

Everyone has run into a rude salesperson at some time or another. Sometimes store salespeople are so rude and so unconcerned that potential customers leave the store without buying something they fully intended to purchase. A rude employee can hurt your sales figures, make your bookstores lose customers, and damage the whole positive atmosphere of your store.

But a knowledgeable, friendly employee becomes a co-bookseller in your bookstore — someone who works with you to help customers connect with the books they will really enjoy. If you pick the right employees, you will have other people who care about your bookstore and the customers who come there, and who will work to make your store a success. So it is vital that you choose carefully.

As you think of the demands of your new store, the niche you are hoping to fill in your community, and the customers you hope to have, make a list of the qualities you want in your employees. Think about the type of person who will be easy for you to work with, who will be warm and helpful to the customers, and who will be an asset to your store.

As you think about the right employee type for your store, consider some of the following qualities of great bookstore employees:

- Honest

- Hardworking

- Responsible

- Reliable

- Friendly

- Knowledgeable

- Polite

- Good sales ability

- Good customer service ability

- Book industry experience

- Educational or niche experience

- Business experience and/or education

- Technology savvy

- Research ability

5.3.2 Recruiting Staff

Now that you know the kind of people you want, you have to find them. There are a number of ways to recruit staff. Both the employment market and where your bookstore is located will affect your experience finding good employees. However, there is definitely a method for finding great employees in every situation.

Classified Advertising

Placing an ad in your local paper's employment section is an excellent way to find good local employees. Make sure your ad is eye-catching and uses just a few words to get the right kind of people through your door. Consider the following ad for a children's bookstore:

> ### Love Kids — Love to Read?
>
> Kidstuff Books in Anytown Mall is looking for a bright, full-time bookseller to join our team. Are you comfortable around children and parents? Do you love helping people? Bookselling or retail experience a plus. Great working environment and good wages. Please fax your resume to 555-1234 or call 555-1000 and ask for Imma Kidd.

Make sure the ad gets the point across quickly. Classified advertising is expensive and is priced by the word. Therefore, it is important to get your point across as quickly as you can. The ad above is 59 words long.

Make sure all the vital information is included. Potential applicants need to know how to contact you or where to fax their resumes. Also, in order to save you lots of time with applicant questions, remember to include the basics about the job in your ad. One important thing to mention is whether the opportunity is full-time or part-time. If you are offering benefits, be sure to mention this important point.

Make sure your ad is correct before it runs in the paper. When you work with an ad rep from your local paper, always ask them to give you a copy of your classified ad as it will appear, so you can check for mistakes. When your ad appears, check it again and make sure it is correct — especially your contact information.

Include words or phrases that quickly help potential applicants find themselves in your ad. In the example above, the title includes the important words "kids" and "reading." Potential applicants who don't really like children and don't enjoy reading will know immediately that the job isn't for them. Those who like children and reading will send you a resume.

When you run an ad, decide ahead of time if you are too busy for phone calls and would prefer the first round of submissions to be sent by fax or email. Taking pre-screening phone calls from applicants is time consuming. Decide what works best for you and your hiring schedule.

Personal Referrals

"I get employees through personal recommendations from people that I trust."

— John Brancati, East End Books
East Hampton, New York

If you talk about your store – and you should, because it's a good way to generate excitement – you can ask everyone you come into contact with if they know someone who would be a good employee. Your regular customers are a good source for referrals, and more than one bookseller has hired a customer to work as an employee. Everyone knows someone who is looking for a job — it never hurts to ask around.

Employment Services

In job markets where there is a low level of unemployment, you may find it necessary to go to an employment agency to help you find potential applicants to hire. These can be found by looking in the Yellow Pages under "Employment" or on the Internet by searching for "Employment Agencies." Agencies typically charge for their services, but they do all the pre-screening and testing for you. You can define exactly the type of applicant you want to see and a representative from an employment agency will set up interview times at your convenience.

Another excellent method to get employees for your bookstore is to buy an ad with any of the many popular online employment service companies. Check out several different companies to find out which one best suits your needs and your hiring budget. The most popular sites are **www.monster.com** and **www.careerbuilder.com**.

5.3.3 The Hiring Process

Screening Resumes

If you run an ad and ask candidates to fax, mail, or email resumes, be prepared to receive more resumes than you might expect. In a period of high unemployment, employers report that sometimes even the smallest ad can result in several hundred resumes.

To screen potential employees, consider the following:

- Personality and personal attributes

- Education and ability

- Professional experience

Personality and Personal Attributes

You won't be able to tell much about someone's personality by looking at their resume, but you can make a few assumptions based on the jobs they have held. For example, resumes that list jobs with heavy customer service and people contact will probably belong to applicants who enjoy working with others.

Education and Ability

People who enjoy books are usually bright. And while you might not demand that the applicants that you screen for your jobs have college degrees, you will be able to tell how they feel about education and learning from how these facts are presented on their resumes.

Professional Experience

What applicants have done in the past definitely has some bearing on whether or not they will be a good fit in your bookstore. Look for applicants with related or complementary experience such as working in retail, membership in a book club, and anything related to your niche. For example, if your store sells fantasy books and the applicant lists gaming as a hobby, they are more likely to be knowledgeable about the products you sell.

The Interview Process

The purpose of an interview is to get to know potential applicants as much as you possibly can in a short length of time.

The best way to conduct an interview is to get the applicants to talk about themselves. Most employers with limited interviewing experience spend too much time talking about the job or their store. And while that is certainly important, it won't help you figure out to whom you are talking and if that person is a good match for your bookstore. A good rule of thumb to follow is that the applicant should do 80 percent of the talking.

Screening applicants on the phone can really help you to decide whom you should see for face-to-face interviews. Listen to more than just what applicants say; listen to how they say it. Are they:

- Friendly?

- Positive?

- Articulate?

- Energetic?

- Confident?

Whether your initial interview is on the phone or in person, have a list of questions prepared in advance. This will keep the process consistent between applicants. You can always add questions that pop up based on their answers as you go along. Here are suggested interview questions from Tom Hennessy, author of the *FabJob Guide to Become a Coffee House Owner.*

"A good first question to ask is why they applied with you in the first place. If they have a sense of humor, they will use it at this point. If they are sincere, they will tell you the truth. If they aren't sure, they will shrug their shoulders and say they don't know.

Here are some other questions to ask:

- Why did you apply to work here?

- What is the ideal schedule you would like to work?

- When can you absolutely not work?

- What sort of experience do you have that you feel qualifies you for this job?

- Tell me about your last job and why you left.

- What was the best job you ever had — the one you had the most fun in?

- Who was your best boss and what made them so great?

- If I talked to someone who worked with you, what would they say about your work habits?

- Do you have any ambitions in this business? If not, what would be your perfect job?"

To get a sense of how an employee will actually behave on the job, it is also a good idea to ask "behavioral questions." Behavioral questions ask applicants to give answers based on their past behavior.

An example is "Tell me about a time you had to deal with a difficult customer. What was the situation and how did you handle it?" Instead of giving hypothetical answers of what someone would do in a particular situation, the applicant must give examples of what they actually have done. While people's behavior can change, past performance is a better indicator of someone's future behavior than hypothetical answers.

References

Another way to learn about an applicant's past behavior is by checking their references. The best references are former employers. (Former co-workers may be friends who will give glowing references no matter how well the employee performed.)

Paying Your New Employees

During the interview process, the issue of pay will come up. You need to know beforehand how much you will pay your new employees. There are legal requirements, such as the national minimum wage, that employers have to take into account when deciding about pay. You should also consider the following things:

- What is normal in the book industry? What other bookstores are paying has bearing on what you will pay. There are industry norms for pay in any business. Find out what a bookstore sales associate (or at least a retail sales associate in a different type of store) is being paid in your city as a guideline to help you decide.

- Is your rate of pay too low? When deciding what to pay your employees, remember that making a pay rate too low will ensure lots of turnover in your store. Turnover means more hiring costs, and hiring employees is expensive, especially if you have to do it often.

- Have you considered required employer contributions? When you determine payroll costs you must add the matched employer contributions for social security and worker's compensation insurance costs to the amount you figure for wages. The current percentage of employer-matched contribution for social security is 7.65% of individual gross wages. See section 4.2.5 for more about worker's compensation costs.

- Have you thought about overtime wages? Retail workers are usually considered nonexempt employees, which means they are eligible to receive overtime wages. Find out what overtime wages will cost your business and see if it's cheaper to hire an extra employee instead.

You will also need to determine costs for unemployment insurance, paid vacations, sick days, holidays or bonuses for employees, and medical benefits, if you should choose to offer them. Also, you must determine if you will set up an employee commission structure.

Many companies will not give you detailed information about a past employee. They are only required to give you employment dates and sometimes they will confirm salary. But many times you will be able to learn a lot about a potential applicant from a reference phone call.

A good employee is often remembered fondly and even asked about by a former employer. An employer may not be able to tell you much about a bad employee for liability reasons, but they can answer the question "Is this employee eligible to be rehired?"

In the *FabJob Guide to Become a Coffee House Owner*, Tom Hennessy relates this story about the importance of checking references:

> "We once had a manager who took off to Hawaii with the weekend deposit. He was eventually caught and the insurance company made a deal with him not to prosecute if he returned the money. About two years later, we received a call from an employer checking on his references. We couldn't believe it; he actually put us down as a reference! We couldn't tell the person checking references that the guy was a thief, but we could say that he was not eligible for rehire."

Here are some other additional questions from Tom Hennessy:

- How long did this person work for you? (This establishes the accuracy of their applications.)

- How well did they get along with everyone? (Looking for team skills.)

- Did they take direction well? (Code words for, "Did they do their job?")

- Could they work independently? (Or did they sit around waiting to be told what to do next?)

- How did they handle stressful situations? (This is important, especially if you are busy.)

If the references make you feel comfortable, call the employee to let them know they have a job and to come in and fill out the paperwork.

5.3.4 New Employees

After you shake hands and say, "The job is yours!", you have to know how to work with the new employee to make sure it is a positive experience for everyone.

New Employee Paperwork

When a new employee is hired there will be paperwork they must fill out. In the U.S. this will be a W-4 and an I-9 form. In Canada, the employee will give you their social insurance number, a T-4, and fill out a Canadian pension form. The U.S. W-4 and Canadian T-4 forms are legal documents verifying how many tax deductions a new employee has.

The amount of tax you will withhold as an employer varies based on the amount of deductions that an employee has. Have the employee fill out the forms, then file them in a folder labelled with their name which you will keep on file.

Check with your state or province's labor office to make sure you are clear about all the forms employees must fill out to work. The sites below give more information on legal paperwork, including where to get blank copies of the forms your employees will need to fill out.

You can purchase a CD full of printable forms for $59.95 through **www.hrlawinfo.com**. Another site, **www.hrdocs.com**, will allow you to download and print any form you need if you purchase a one-year subscription to their site that starts at $39.99. For Canadian readers, the Human Resources Department Canada allows you to download and print forms for free through their website at **www100.hrdc.gc.ca/ e_formshome.shtml**.

Employee Emergency Contact Card

If the unexpected happens, as it sometimes will, you want to be prepared. Having employees fill out an emergency card for their file will help you contact their doctor, spouse, or other friends or family members in case of an emergency. Besides being the most rational and human thing to do, being prepared in this way can safeguard you against liability.

Make sure every employee's emergency card contains the following:

- Their correct and updated address and phone number

- Their family doctor and choice of hospital

- Any medications taken

- Allergies or special medical conditions

- The name and phone number of a family member emergency contact

- The name and phone number of an alternate emergency contact

Make sure that the emergency cards for staff, including one for you, are filled out and placed in alphabetical order in a filing cabinet or another location, and that everyone who works with you knows where this information is kept. Ask employees to verify that their emergency information is correct and updated as soon as it changes.

Employee Handbook

As mentioned in section 5.1.2, it's a good idea to develop an employee handbook containing the rules and policies that you want your bookstore staff to follow. Hand it out with a page that the employee is to read, sign, and return to you by their first day of work stating that they understand your bookstore policies and rules and agree to follow them.

New Employee Orientation

While an employee handbook can give your new employee valuable information, it is not enough to prepare them for working in your store.

Showing up on the first day of a new job is stressful for any employee. The new employees you hire are full of hope and anxiety, and are trying their best to make a good impression and be successful in your eyes. You should do your best to make them feel welcome and appreciated.

Perhaps the best way to illustrate how negative a first day on the job can be is to tell a true story of an experience I once had. I was hired for a new job at a highly recommended company. I was very excited about the position and the pay — I felt like it would be a perfect opportunity for me. I arrived on the appointed day, ten minutes early, and was greeted by a receptionist who told me that she would put me temporarily in an office and that the Operations Manager would be in to meet with me shortly.

Three hours later, I was still sitting unobtrusively in a small office waiting for the Operations Manager, who never showed up. I read and reread the brief employment forms I was given to fill out and waited. Finally, not really knowing what to do, I ventured to the main office and tapped on the door of a Vice President. She was surprised I had waited, said something very negative about the Operations Manager, and asked a coworker to help me get settled.

My new coworker was working on a totally frantic and unrealistic deadline and I was enlisted to help her. She handed me a massive pile of confusing work and said, "Anything you can do to help will be something." Then she left.

Three and a half hours later the Operations Manager appeared. I had already been given work but no place to sit and no computer to use to complete the work. Eventually, right before lunch, my new coworker said I could sit at her workstation and she would move somewhere else.

Another employee asked me for help so I got up to try to help her. While I did this the frazzled coworker on deadline ran back to her workstation, took the work she had given me, and stormed off. When I went back to collect the work, she was angry that I had not understood the seriousness of the deadline.

I stayed at this company for five months and there was never a day that I was trained, received any formal orientation, or was made to feel welcome or comfortable. In retrospect, I believe I should have walked out after the Operations Manager was three hours late for our first meeting.

Although I was not employed as a bookseller, many of the things that went wrong are typical oversights in the case of any employer. There are many things you can learn from this experience when it comes to planning your new employee's first day:

Show Respect

Show your new employee the same respect that you expect to receive. This means that you, or the person you have designated to greet a new employee, should be on hand at the exact time you schedule. Making anyone wait for hours is simply rude and says, "You don't matter."

Make Definite Plans

Make definite orientation plans for your new employee. Develop a list of what you will show and tell your employee, and go through each point. Plan for the employee to have lunch with you or a friendly coworker on the first day. Remember that new work situations can be very uncomfortable. Orientation is designed to give a new employee a point of reference and direction about their new experience.

Start Out Slowly

While you are explaining procedures and the details of your store, don't expect your brand new employee to be able to jump right in. Realize that the first few days in your bookstore will be a time for your new employee to acclimate, to learn, and to become comfortable.

Don't Overwhelm Them

Don't throw your new employee into the fire. Starting them out on the day of the biggest sale in your store's history is a bad idea. Choose a time that is relatively slow-paced to let your new employee learn in a calm environment.

Keep Training

After a new employee's first day, assign a veteran employee to work with them and answer any questions they may have. Assigning a friendly peer trainer gives a new employee someone to go to for help.

Check in Often

Once your employee has been working for a few days, schedule an informal meeting to check in. Ask them to voice questions, comments, and possible concerns. Offer some positive feedback about your new employee's performance.

Taking the time to make sure your new employee feels comfortable and positive working in your bookstore will pay off in the long run. Happy employees who feel positive about what they are doing often become long-term assets for your bookstore.

Keep Informed

The government has many laws that protect workers in the workplace. It is important to be aware of these laws and to make sure that your bookstore abides by them. Also, ensuring compliance with all workplace laws will help you protect your bookstore from the occasional disgruntled employee.

The U.S. and Canadian governments have websites which provide information on almost any issue concerning employment law. Make sure to check how these laws affect your bookstore and how you can abide by them.

- *U.S. Department of Labor*
  www.dol.gov

- *Laws and Regulations (Canada)*
  (Click on "Labour Law at a Glance" once you select a language at the main site.)
  www.hrmanagement.gc.ca

5.4 Opening Day

Can you believe it? You are ready to open your new bookstore! After months of preparation, planning, and hard work, today will be the first day you meet customers and sell books to them. And while you will definitely not have all the kinks ironed out, you will be in business!

Take a deep breath and remember to do just one thing at a time, be prepared for things to not go as planned, and keep your sense of humor. You are a success today. No matter how the day goes, you have achieved your dream — you have opened your own bookstore! From this day forward all you have to do is learn to run your store and make it profitable! But if you have come this far, you certainly have the talent, ability, and drive to make it as a bookseller. Congratulations!

Things to Check Before You Open Your Doors

A few days before you open for the first time, there are definitely things to check on and prepare. Take a look at the list below to make sure you are ready.

Your Physical Store

❑ Does your store look ready?

❑ Are the displays attractive and finished?

❑ Are your restrooms ready for visitors?

❑ Do you have backup paper products?

❑ Are your floors, windows, and other surface areas clean?

❑ Are your bookshelves dusted and are the books neatly displayed?

❑ Are your displays and feature displays ready and inviting?

❑ Are your window displays ready and inviting?

❑ If you have a café or food area, is it stocked?

❑ Are the staff trained and practiced?

❑ Have you planned your opening menu?

❑ Have the people preparing the food had a trial run?

❑ Do you have a staff member prepared to help customers purchase food?

Inventory

❑ Are your books priced?

❑ Are your books all on the shelves?

❑ If you have books in your warehouse or storage area, are they organized for you to get them as you need them?

❑ Is your inventory software ready?

❑ Are all the books entered into the system?

❑ Does staff know how to use it?

❑ Do you know who is responsible for keeping the shelves orderly and stocked?

Safety

❑ Do you have your keys?

❑ Do you know how to work your burglar alarm?

❑ Is the code for the burglar alarm set?

❑ Do you have working fire extinguishers?

❑ Do you have keys to emergency exits?

❑ Are they ready to be opened during business?

❑ Do you have emergency numbers posted by at least one telephone for 911, the fire department, a local hospital, your landlord's number, etc.?

Procedures

❑ Is your cash wrap area ready?

❑ Do you have cash in the cash drawer to make change?

❏ Are your computers working?

❏ Do you have staff working today?

❏ Have you gone over the basics of how you want your staff to handle:

    ❏ Sales?

    ❏ Accepting checks and credit cards?

    ❏ Making change?

    ❏ Answering customer questions?

    ❏ Helping customers find books and sidelines in the store?

    ❏ Bagging books and sidelines?

    ❏ Handing out promotional material?

    ❏ Handing out grand opening invitations?

    ❏ Giving new customers information about upcoming events?

❏ Have you figured out your employees' schedules?

❏ Have you decided on lunch breaks?

❏ Do you have your hours planned?

❏ Do you have special opening day/week hours?

❏ Do you have an open/closed sign?

❑ Do you know who is in charge of closing the cash register for the day?

❑ Do you know who counts the receipts?

❑ Do you know who will be responsible for the banking?

❑ Do you know who cleans and prepares the store for the next day?

Technology

❑ Are your computers working the way you want them to?

❑ Is your Internet access working?

❑ Are staff members prepared to use the computers?

❑ Does your fax machine work?

❑ Is it hooked up?

❑ Does someone know how to use it?

❑ Does your phone system work?

❑ Is your answering machine in place?

❑ Is there a recording on it that announces your opening and gives hours and directions?

Marketing and Advertising

❑ Did you send press releases announcing your opening?

❑ Did you talk to the newspaper and possibly the local news about getting someone over to your store to do a story?

❑ Did you send out flyers?

❑ Did you send out email announcements?

❑ Did you contact a local radio station about broadcasting from your store as a promotion for your opening week?

Memorable Additions

❑ Do you have your camera?

❑ Will you take pictures of your new staff?

❑ Will you have someone videotape a portion of opening day?

❑ Will you have a cake or a bottle of champagne to have a small celebration with staff and make them feel excited about working at your new bookstore?

❑ Will you take a moment to enjoy this amazing, unrepeatable day?

Some Final Thoughts on the First Few Days

Any time you do something new, especially when a number of people are involved, there will be problems and mistakes. Prepare for these.

Make sure to meet with staff after you close for the first time and talk over what went right and what could be improved. Make changes and fine tune what you are doing on a daily basis.

When you go home at night, or have a moment to review your thoughts, make plans for the following day. Make sure to keep meeting with staff frequently in the first few days to hear how everything is going and make additional changes to your procedures.

5.5 Marketing Your Bookstore

Marketing – the great art of getting people excited enough about your bookstore to come in and buy – is vital in today's book industry. This section covers a variety of techniques to market your bookstore and get those customers from the first day you open.

5.5.1 Advertising

Smart booksellers know that book customers are wooed, they are informed, and they are actively pursued to come into bookstores through advertising. Even before you open the doors of your bookstore for the first time, you can use advertising to create a "buzz" and generate some excitement and anticipation about your new store.

To decide where to advertise, you'll need to know what target market you want to go after. This is where a marketing plan (see section 3.5.2) can be particularly helpful.

Newspapers and Magazines

Consider specialty magazines for your area that pertain to your bookstore's niche. For example, if you own a children's bookstore, you might want to advertise in a local parenting magazine.

Most communities have free give-away advertising papers or magazines directed at parents that are usually distributed in local businesses. Read a magazine or newspaper carefully to see if an advertisement for your bookstore would fit with the theme of the paper, the articles, and the other ads.

Next, consider the proper section of your local paper. Is it possible to run your ad in the arts or book review section? Talk with your newspaper advertising representative and find out.

Many publications will provide you with a free media kit with lots of important demographic information about their readership. This information will help you determine if their readers are the sort of customers you are looking for and if it is the right publication for your ad.

Some publications will design your ad for free, while others will design it for an additional cost and give you a copy of the ad to run elsewhere.

Your ad should describe a service, event, or offer that makes you stand out from your competition, and focus on the customers' wants and needs. Customers are more likely to be impressed with a bookstore that promises "difficult to find titles" than "thousands of titles." After all, your customer is not looking to buy thousands of titles!

It has been estimated that many people need to see an advertisement three to seven times before they buy, so running an ad once may not give you as much business as you would hope. A small ad run every week for a couple of months can generate more business than a single full page ad. To test the effectiveness of each ad you could include a coupon that expires by a particular date.

Radio and Television

When was the last time you heard an ad on radio or saw a television commercial encouraging you to visit a local bookstore?

Most bookstore owners do not advertise on radio and TV because broadcast ads don't come close to generating the type of results you can get from advertising in print publications. There's a logical reason for this — people who see your ad in a newspaper or magazine are readers. In addition to reading periodicals, they are more likely to buy and read books than people who get most of their information from broadcast media.

However, you might consider broadcast advertising if you are holding an event that you think will interest a wide audience, such as a visit by a celebrity author. Contact local stations to find out their advertising rates and audience.

Advertising can be expensive, so consider approaching them instead for free publicity or to see if they want to become a "media sponsor" of your event (i.e. to provide free or discounted ads in return for being recognized at the event with a banner or logo in your print ads).

Suggestions for getting free publicity are covered later in this section.

Yellow Pages

Yellow Pages ads can help you attract people from outside of your immediate area, particularly if you have a specialty bookstore. Take a look at Yellow Pages ads for other bookstores to get ideas. You can either design the ad yourself, have the Yellow Pages design it for you, or hire a designer.

If you are interested in advertising, contact your local Yellow Pages to speak with a sales rep. Check the print version of your phone book for contact information.

5.5.2 Events

Events are some of the most enjoyable moments you can have in your own bookstore.

If you like parties and like to interact with others, having events in your bookstore can give you a festive, happy atmosphere that your customers will love. Pat Tegtmeier, owner of A Novel View in Anchorage, Alaska, described a successful event:

> "A Novel View recently co-sponsored a "business exchange" block party, in which all the members of the Anchorage Convention and Visitors Bureau were invited. There was a band in the street, refreshments at each business around the block, and the participants had little passports to take to each business to get stamped and enter a drawing for prizes. This successful event brought about 200 people into the store over a two-hour period (more than we usually have in three weeks!), and as a result brought many into the store who never knew we existed. It was our best book sale day in the year-and-a-half that we have been in our location."

Events that you host in your bookstore will accomplish a lot of things. They:

- Bring new business to your bookstore

- Attract attention to your bookstore

- Help you create a name for your store

- Give customers a sense of community

- Help you build relationships with authors

- Allow you to network and form business alliances with other small business owners in the community

- Provide a catalyst for giving back to the community through supporting a charitable organization as part of an event

- Let people know that you are open for business!

Your Grand Opening

Having a grand opening is a perfect way to announce to the world, the book customers in your area, and the press that you are open and in business. It is a way to celebrate your promising future, and a way of bringing together other book professionals, your friends, colleagues, and the community. It is a wonderful way to generate excitement.

It is also a way of celebrating your success. When you get to the moment of your grand opening you will know that you have successfully done mountains of preparation. You have learned how to run a business, you have gotten financing, found and organized a space, and learned everything you need to know to make it possible to open your doors for business. It is a reason to celebrate.

Scheduling Your Grand Opening

The best thing to do is to begin with a calendar date and then brainstorm what you will need to do to make the event happen.

It is always best to schedule your grand opening for sometime after you have opened your doors. On your opening day, there won't be time to work out all the little (and big) disasters that always occur when a new business opens.

Give yourself and your staff time to work out the bugs and get used to your new store. Hopefully by the time you have your grand opening, everyone will know where everything is, your staff will have had practice making suggestions and helping customers locate books they want, and all the ordinary mechanics of running your store will be worked out.

Making Your Event Fit Your Customers

Before you plan your grand opening, you will need to determine how much money you would like to budget for this event.

In the case of the East End Bookstore, owner John Brancati positioned his bookstore in an affluent community and chose to make his grand opening a gala. His clientele expected an event similar to the other sorts of events that they attend in this upscale community, so his planning and his budget reflected this expectation.

You may find that your community and your budget is far different, and that is fine. It is appropriate to have the kind of grand opening event that will be a comfortable fit for the customers you want to attract.

For example, if you open a children's bookstore you will want to frame your event around your number one customer — kids. A fancy catering job will be completely lost on children; however, they would probably love a live appearance of a costumed book character, or a magician, or a children's author who would read from a popular children's book.

Keep in mind what your customers will enjoy and what will make them excited about your store. A travel bookstore might give away a cruise as a grand opening event door prize. A college town bookstore might offer a semester's worth of books as a raffle prize.

If you want to get media coverage of your event, you'll need to do something interesting. For example, if you have a celebrity that will attend, or a number of wonderful authors, or you coordinate your event as one that sponsors an important charity or civic organization with a donation, you will have a better chance of getting the press involved.

> **TIP:** Have a backup plan for an outdoor event or any other event that might be pre-empted because of weather. Consider all the possibilities before you decide to host an outdoor event.

Appearances

Guest appearances are always a wonderful way to get customers excited about your store, and a grand opening event is no exception. Authors enjoy doing book signings and making appearances because it helps them sell their books.

To arrange author appearances, contact their publishers' publicity departments. Make sure your authors are available and confirmed for the day you select. Find out what special things they need or what special accommodations are necessary to help make their appearance in your store incredible.

Food

Plan a menu. Decide ahead of time how elaborate or simple you want to be. In the case of a gala sort of grand opening, you will probably want the event to be catered. For a less formal event, you might just serve coffee and desserts. Make sure to have food that will be easy to serve, keep well in a buffet setting, and appeal to a variety of different preferences.

Consider what sort of food you are serving and where. Don't serve barbequed ribs around your modern first editions! Have an area for food that isn't close enough to your books to damage them in case of an accidental spill.

Music and Entertainment

Music can really help set the mood at your grand opening event. If you sell music CDs as part of your sidelines, consider featuring the CD of a local musician and ask the musician to play your event in exchange for free publicity and the chance to sell their music at the same time.

Consider how you want entertainment to be viewed at your event. Do you want it to be something that people will enjoy, but be part of the background? Or will you set up a stage and use it for entertainment, announcements, and possibly a door prize drawing?

Remember to consider your audience when selecting entertainment. Entertainment should be enjoyable, not distracting or annoying, and appropriate to the audience in attendance.

Door Prizes

One excellent idea for door prizes is book gift certificates. This way the winners will return to your store and you can begin to build customer relationships.

Another great tie in is gifts that relate to the specialty or focus of your bookstore. A bookstore that features healing and new age books might give away a spa certificate. A mystery store could give away tickets for a popular mystery theater show.

Also, many other business owners are happy to give away promotional gift certificates. Consider trading a gift certificate from your business in exchange for a gift certificate from another business.

Invitations

Invitations can be elaborate or simple. You can send them out in regular mail or you can send email invitations — or you can use both methods.

If you are hosting an exclusive gala grand opening with a sit-down dinner, you need to know how many people will actually attend your event. One way to get a sense of who will attend your event is to require reservations.

Who should you invite, and how will you let them know about the event? There are a number of ways to determine who will be on your guest list, but consider including the following:

- Everyone you know. Invite all your friends, your family, and your professional contacts. Include everyone you have ever talked to about your bookstore.

- The community. Make sure to advertise your grand opening event.

- The press. Contact local newspapers, radio, and television stations. See section 5.4.3 for advice on how to contact the media.

During the Event

Hosting an event in your bookstore is sort of like having a really big party in your own home. You want to make sure people are comfortable, have fun, get enough to eat, and enjoy themselves.

You should spend a few minutes with people you know and introduce yourself to people you don't know. In short, hosting a great event requires that you are a good host.

Get your bookstore staff involved with you as co-hosts for the event. Make sure you have enough staff working to make people involved in the event feel like it is organized and that their needs are being met.

Schedule the necessary staff to work the cash wrap area and ring up those sales! Remember, one of the main reasons for hosting in-store events is to bring you additional business!

More Event Ideas

In addition to your grand opening event, consider some of these ideas:

- Book signings

- Children's story time

- Wine and cheese party as a celebration planned around a new wine book or another cook or gourmet book

- Murder mystery party to herald the release of a new mystery or suspense novel

- Christmas party with a charitable co-theme

- Business networking lunches with discounts on business titles

- Come as a favorite book character party for kids (or adults)

- Seminars on absolutely any subject that an author has written a new book on

- Craft classes

- Book clubs

- Health screenings or blood donation events

- Holiday fair or bazaar in coordination with other retailers in your area

- Retailer "block party"

- Retailer midnight sale or sidewalk sale

- Back to school event

- Any event to celebrate a city event or state or national holiday or simultaneous celebration

- Art show — hang the work of a local painter and hold a first night event

- New Year's Eve alternative for parents and kids

One exceptional book signing I attended in the last year was at the Changing Hands Bookstore in Tempe, Arizona. I took my nine-year-old to see her favorite author, Barbara Parks. Parks is the author of a series of popular chapter books for early readers based on the madcap and hilarious adventures of little Junie B. Jones. My daughter and several hundred other children all waited patiently in line for a chance to meet Barbara Park and have their books signed.

Changing Hands organized the event in a really handy and relaxing way. They asked people waiting for Barbara Parks to take a number and then browse or go to the café until their number was called. While we were waiting we found some other books we wanted, had a snack, and naturally bought a Junie B. Jones book for an autograph.

All in all it was a wonderful experience. Barbara Parks was personable and lovely to each child (and their parents, too) and we all felt like we had a truly special experience.

Working with a Publicist

For some booksellers, a publicist is the way to go. A publicist can help you organize all the aspects of your grand opening and help you get the press and people you want there. Some booksellers choose to hire a publicist for the first several months of their new venture to help them get their businesses off the ground. Depending on your budget and your niche, this may be a good choice for you.

5.5.3 Free Publicity

Any time you can plan a newsworthy event, you create an opportunity to generate free newspaper, radio, or television publicity for your bookstore.

Pre-Event Publicity

To get free publicity for an upcoming event, submit a summary of your event details (date, time, theme, cost,what's happening, etc.) to any upcoming events columns in local newspapers and magazines. Most local radio community TV stations have public service announcements about upcoming local events. Check with the stations to see how to have your bookstore's upcoming events mentioned on the air.

Also ask any authors who are scheduled to appear at your event if they are willing to do media interviews. If so, contact local media newspapers to let them know the author is coming to town and is available for an interview before the event. You can phone, fax, or send a news release (also called a "press release") to the editor of the appropriate section of the newspaper. Depending on the author, that might be the Books section, Business section, Lifestyle section, or another part of the paper. If the editor's name is not published in the paper, you can call and ask the receptionist.

For radio, contact talk show producers, news directors, or morning show hosts, depending on who you think would be most interested in your topic. When you contact them, emphasize how much the show's audience will benefit from an interview. Keep in mind that they are not interested in giving you free advertising – their goal is to improve their ratings, so anyone they interview should be dynamic and interesting.

Also, keep in mind that many station employees are overworked and underpaid. If you can make their job easier you are much more likely to land an interview. The best way to make their job easier is to email or fax them a list of "frequently asked questions."

Writing a News Release

News releases are written to get the media excited about your event – excited enough that they will mention your event in their publication or cover it on their show. The writing should be crisp, cover all the vital information about the event highlights, and point out why the event is important. Here are some tips for writing a news release:

- Give your press release a strong lead paragraph that answers the six main questions: who, what, where, when, why, and how.

- Include factual information about the event. A press release should read like a news story, not an advertisement.

- Keep it short. Aim for a maximum of 500 words.

- Include contact information at the end of the press release so that reporters and readers can get tickets.

Look at this fictional news release to see how information is presented:

Sample News Release

Contact:
Grace Jasmine
Grace's Book Gallery
123 Success Street
Bookreader, CA 12345
Phone: (123) 456-7890
Email: gracesbookgallery@aol.com

FOR IMMEDIATE RELEASE   12/01/05

**Author Penny Foryurthots Heads List of Celebs
at Grace's Book Gallery Grand Opening Gala**

Highly acclaimed author, Penny Foryurthots, who has written this season's smash how-to guide, *Making Your Own Money*, is coming to the popular new booklover's meeting place, Grace's Book Gallery in Bookreader, California.

Foryurthots will appear from 10:00 a.m. to 7:00 p.m. on December 24, 2005, to help bookstore owner Grace Jasmine celebrate the opening of her new bookstore, Grace's Book Gallery.

Foryurthots will be one of several authors slated to discuss her new bestselling book as well as sign copies for fans. Other authors scheduled to appear include Ty Priter, author of *Finger Pecking Your Way to Financial Success*, and Rich Erthanue, author of *Big Bucks for Small Minds*.

Grace's Book Gallery owner Grace Jasmine has created her treasure of a bookstore with an emphasis on nonfiction titles dealing with money management, investment, finance and get-rich-quick schemes. Her store boasts the only collection of children's finance and investment nonfiction topics west of the Mississippi. She calls this section the "Yuppie Youth Section" in a salute to the mid-eighties "Me Generation" lingo.

Ten percent of the gala's sales proceeds will be donated to the Community Literacy Campaign. Mayor Tom Reynolds will be on hand to receive a check and meet with citizens of the community for a question and answer session about how to get kids to read in a video game-obsessed world. All children's books will be "buy one get one free" the day of the gala grand opening.

Foryurthots, Priter and Erthanue will take part in a free panel discussion, "Easy Money," at 5:00 p.m. Seating is limited and reservations are suggested. Come early to browse this season's best in popular finance nonfiction and sip a cappuccino in Grace's Booklovers Café. Live music and a surprise guest or two will round out the event. The first 100 people through the door will receive a free "Reading for Dollars" backpack.

Grace's Book Gallery is located at 123 Success Street in Bookreader, California, right across the street from Bookreader's City Hall. Call Grace's Book Gallery for information and reservations at 123-456-7890, or visit the store's website at www.gracesbookgallery.com and start making money today!

Invite the Media to the Event

To get media to cover an event at your bookstore, contact the assignment editor at TV stations, the news director at radio stations, and the appropriate editors at magazines and newspapers.

A good way to invite the media is by sending a media advisory. This is a one page document which you can fax, email or mail. A sample template appears below, courtesy of Real-World PR (**www. realworldpr.com**).

The more interesting your event is, the better your chance of the press showing up. Sometimes radio stations will send a radio disk jockey to a business to broadcast live during an event.

Sample Media Advisory Format

For Immediate Release

* * * MEDIA ALERT * * *
* * * PHOTO OPPORTUNITY * * *

[Headline Goes Here, Initial Capped, Bold and Centered]

WHAT: [A brief description of the event goes here]

WHO: [Key players in event]

WHEN: [Date, day of week, and start and end times of event]

WHERE: [Location and address and site location go here]

BACKGROUND: [Additional background about event goes here (if necessary) or company boilerplate (a brief description of the company, and any information you want readers to know about it, such as what type of business it is in, what its annual sales are, where it is headquartered, where branch offices are located, the number of employees, etc.)]

\# \# \#

For more information, contact:
[contact information goes here]

Talk with radio stations about doing that for some of your events. Think about how a live broadcasted event from your store might look, and what authors you could invite to be celebrity speakers.

Likewise, the way to get television coverage is to have such amazing events with well-known authors that it becomes news. When you schedule a well-known author to appear in your store, contact local news stations well before the event and find out if they will send a person to cover it. The more "hot" the author is, the better chance you will have of getting some television news coverage. Also, consider your city's local cable station. Many cities have local cable stations that feature some kind of a city events show — see if this might be a place to start.

Also, while it isn't "professional" television programming, don't overlook the many universities and colleges, and even some high schools, that have film classes and student-run television stations. Students will come and film for free and perhaps even give you a tape of an event. This might be another great way to spread the word about your store without destroying your advertising budget.

5.5.4 Your Bookstore's Internet Presence

Do you remember back in the dark ages before 1990 when the Internet was not the single most important business tool around? There was a time when the World Wide Web was brand new and even accessing a web page was an adventure. The idea of building a web page was a glory dream of computer programmers and college students in information technology classes. Regular business owners just didn't do it.

As time went on, websites became all the rage. Once the initial excitement was over, businesspeople and consumers began to see that, the Internet is certainly a viable and here-to-stay way to do business and to advertise. It is, and always will be, an opportunity for more customers, more exposure to a global audience who would have never heard of your bookstore in an age without the Internet. The Internet is a fantastic opportunity for your bookstore to thrive, 24 hours a day.

The Benefits of an Online Presence

What used to be called a company website in less sophisticated days is now referred to as an "Internet presence." Being present on the Internet is really the only way to go for "brick and mortar" bookstores today, and it is a good idea for many reasons. There are a number of reasons your bookstore will benefit by having an Internet presence.

Readers Use the Internet

You found this book because you are Internet savvy and you use the Internet to find out things to support your life, your career, and your aspirations. And you are not alone. People who buy books use the Internet, and you want to make sure they find your store.

Everyone Else is There

Every business that you will be in direct competition with has an Internet presence. This goes for everyone from the superstores – Amazon, Barnes and Noble, and Borders – to the independent booksellers in your area. The Internet is quickly becoming the most easily accessible and convenient business marketplace. Not only do people buy books on the Internet, but they also get information about where they want to go and get the details online beforehand.

The most important potential benefits for your bookstore are two-fold — you can attract customers to your store, and you can sell to customers online. Having a web presence makes your business accessible. It's a high-tech advertisement that can have all the bells and whistles you want.

Low-Cost Advertising

Advertising can be expensive. Advertising space in a local newspaper can be amazingly costly and it appears only for a short time. Flyers, catalogs, and other printed materials require paper, printing costs, and postage. Once a flyer is mailed to your potential customer base, it is gone forever. If a mailed ad is not read and used by a potential customer, it is simply discarded. Your advertising dollars can easily go down the drain.

But with an Internet presence, for a reasonable monthly fee, you can have 24-hour-a-day advertising designed to get people excited about your bookstore. If you have an online store as part of your site, you can sell books to customers while you are sleeping.

Reach an International Customer Base

Customers on the Internet are sitting in front of their computer screens in homes and offices all around the world. Having an Internet presence gives you instant access to an international customer base.

Book-loving tourists planning their vacations to your part of the world can find out about your store and include it in their travel itineraries. Online book shoppers can buy from your online store no matter where they are in the world.

Give Your Physical Customers a Virtual Bookstore Home

Your customers need a place to connect to their favorite store online. After they have enjoyed spending an afternoon in your store, they can sit at home and read your recommendations or book reviews for their next purchase. They can sign up for your monthly email newsletter. You can even organize online book clubs or discussion groups.

Your physical customers can find out about upcoming events on your website. They can see which authors will be coming to your store for signings, and they can find out information about when new books will be on your shelves. They can stay connected to your bookstore and thinking about and planning for their next visit while they are at home.

Creating Your Website

Just like you began the process of determining the type of real life bookstore you wanted by examining already existing bookstores in your area, you need to browse bookstore sites online, too. One excellent source for this is the American Booksellers Association website's list of member bookstores at **www.bookweb.org/bookstores/browse.html**.

Here are some features to include in your own bookstore's website to help you get started:

- Your bookstore's name and address

- A photograph of the front of your store

- Directions to your store

- Store hours

- Parking around your store

- Upcoming events and a calendar

- Text and pictures of recent store events

- Gift certificate information

- Book club information

- Information about signing up for your email newsletter and an online website form to do so

- Your email contact information

- Reviews and information about new and interesting books

- Information about your staff

You can set this up using your web design software. If the technical details of web page programming are a little beyond you – and you are not alone – consider getting a techno-savvy friend to help you do this or buy a couple of hours of "techie" consulting time from a computer geek. There are many qualified companies and individual consultants who can help you to create an excellent website.

It is important to have someone on your bookstore staff who has the ability to change and update the website. Bookstore owners update their websites frequently to advertise and promote events and inform customers about other exciting in-store news.

BookSense.com

BookSense is a program that is open to any American Booksellers Association member with a physical location. By joining the BookSense program you affiliate yourself with other booksellers across the country and gain access to a search engine database for books that will instantly help you to create your site and generate online sales.

When booksellers choose to create a BookSense.com Internet presence, their customers instantly have access to a book-buying database that rivals any superstore anywhere. The little guys – independent booksellers – have taken the energy of the Internet and formed a successful collective. And according to Oren Teicher, Chief Operating Officer of the American Booksellers Association, the system is working.

Booksellers swear by the success of this Internet-based service. It is an excellent way to add a cohesive identity to your website with the clout of this important national organization. By the way, if you have not yet joined the ABA just this service alone is an excellent reason to join. Besides being able to link and identify your website with the BookSense program there are many more benefits, all discussed on the program's website at **www.bookweb.org/booksense/dotcom**.

Begin by looking at other members' sites and see how they have set them up. While the BookSense logo and search engine give them all continuity, you will see that each bookseller has created their own identity — because independent bookstores, like snowflakes, are never identical. Bookmark the ones you particularly like and review them in depth.

After paying a one-time setup fee of $350 and a $225 per month subscription fee for a BookSense.com website, members' websites can be up and running within days. Members have access to their administrative pages 24/7. The website administrative tools are set up so that bookstore owners don't need to have sophisticated Internet skills to make a website. This gives people enormous leeway. They can do as much as they want, or as much as they can — it's entirely up to them.

Advertising Your Website

When done correctly, the Internet can be a great source of 24-hour-a-day advertising. When done incorrectly, your website won't attract much attention. It is therefore important to get the word out about your website. Let people who come into your store know you have a site, and mention your website address in every other piece of advertising or written material you create about your store.

Some web search engines sell ad space that works when people are using the search engine to search for something in your category. One such service is Google's AdWords (**http://adwords.google.com**). This service allows you to create your own ad, and pay for it only when someone actually clicks on it. There are a variety of ways to set up your ad using international, national, and even regional parameters. And each time a user searches using the keywords you select you will get your store's name in front of more potential customers.

5.5.5 Your Email Newsletter

One of the great benefits for booksellers in technology is the ability to use email for advertising. Email is free, you don't have to print anything, you don't have to leave the store to go to the post office, and you don't have to pay for stamps. Using email to its best advantage is something that all but the most resistant booksellers do these days.

Getting an Emailing List

Creating an email address list of customers to send your newsletter to will be an ongoing project. Make it known that your store has not only a wonderful Internet presence, but a helpful monthly newsletter designed to keep busy customers informed about upcoming events, author signings in your store, and vital information that they need as readers to remain aware of what books are new and hot.

Add to your email address book by doing the following:

- Put a notice about your email newsletter in every ad you run in print

- Pass out flyers with purchases to ask customers to check out your website and sign up for your email newsletter

- Design your website so that customers visiting you online will be able to sign up for the newsletter on your website

Writing Your Monthly Newsletter

Now it's time to put your own hidden literary talents to work and write your own email newsletter. And don't worry if you would rather sell a book than write one, an email newsletter doesn't have to be a great masterpiece — it is meant to inform and educate the potential customer and reader about what is going on in your store and what books are new and hot.

Take a look at a typical email newsletter kindly provided for this book by Pat Tegtmeier, owner of A Novel View in Anchorage, Alaska:

A Novel View Bookstore Newsletter: February 2004

A Novel View
415 L Street
Anchorage, AK 99501
Phone: (907) 278-0084

A Novel View Bookstore: A Small Shop of Great Books

It may be snowy and cold outside, but it's toasty and comfy inside. With February in mind, we'd like to remind you that we have thousands of love stories to warm your heart. And we'll offer a sweet surprise to each person who comes into A Novel View on Valentine's Day, February 14, between 10:00 a.m. and 5:00 p.m.

Art Receptions

First Friday ArtWalk — February

James Morris of SunJam Studios will be this month's featured artist, beginning with a First Friday ArtWalk reception on February 6th, from 6:00 to 8:00 p.m. His exhibit, "Unique Artwork with an Alaskan Touch," includes photo-perfect renderings of aircraft, as well as whimsical perspectives such as his "Alaskan Road Trip."

James moved to Alaska in 1991 to pursue his artwork and to enjoy the beauty and wonders of the Great Land. He has been drawing since he was five years old after being inspired by his mother, who was a commercial artist.

 A self-taught artist, James took art in seventh and eighth grade with no other formal training. He has been a freelance artist for the past 20 years, winning numerous art awards. He draws primarily in pen and ink (color and black and white) and also uses airbrush technique. Says James: "My vision of the natural beauty of Alaska and its wildlife is reflected in my work for you to enjoy. All of my art comes from my heart and it is my great pleasure to share it with you!"

First Friday ArtWalk — March

March is "Youth Art Month," when we will honor budding artists at a First Friday ArtWalk reception on March 5th from 6:00 to 8:00 p.m., through a School-Business Partnership with Theresa Heckart's students from Central Middle School.

Selected Books of the Month

Funny Business in the Kitchen

Just in: *A Politically Correct Cookbook*, by Catherine Daniel Vonderahe. This clever 153-page spiral-bound creation was cooked up as a kitchen guide for the 90's, when "candidates traversed the land... and promises dripped like honey from the candidates' lips, feeding the hungry masses at countless rallies." How relevant today, as we face another campaign year.

"This book is a work of fiction," notes the author. "The dishes described in this culinary work are meant to be served with a grain of salt and consumed with the tongue planted firmly in the cheek." Some sample recipes:

- Campaign Trail Baloney [a cheese spread]
- Surgeon General's Wiener Wraps and "Condo"-ments
- Senator Ted Kennedy's Party Punch
- Antonin Scalia's Meatballs in Your Court
- Eggs McBaghdad
- Endangered Reeses

Whether you're a cookbook collector, humorist, political-savvy constituent, or teacher, this book will spark lively conversations! This gem of humor and recipes is spiced wth imaginative illustrations and politically correct quizzes and puzzles.

Best Selling Authors

Books by popular novelists are always available at A Novel View at half the original cover price. Thanks to our customers, today's best-seller may be on our bookshelves tomorrow!

Great Books of the Month

Amy Tan's birthday falls on February 19th, and we're pleased to carry some of her books in our Literature section, which begins at the top of the stairs on the second floor.

Collectible of the Month

Among our treasured collectible books is *The Testimony of the Rocks*, by Hugh Miller, published in 1857, and priced at $10. This unique volume is a compilation of lectures presented at the Edinburgh Philosophical Institution between 1852-1855, in which the author attempts to reconcile natural science with the Biblical views of creation.

Education

Better Math in 5 Minutes a Day sounds too good to be true. Written by Fran Gibson, a teacher who has conducted math workshops around the country, this 136-page soft-bound book is intended to enhance intermediate-age children's understanding of math.

The book includes multiplication, division, fractions, and decimals, along with Parents' Corner comments, Teaching Tips, exercises, riddles and illustrations that appeal to kids. A sample:

> **Question:** How can you divide six potatoes evenly among 20 people?
>
> **Answer:** Boil and mash them!

Education is one of about 55 categories of books in the store.

Biography

Our Biography shelves murmur life stories of both the well-known and the obscure. One recent arrival is *Will Rogers: A Biography*, by journalist and English professor Ben Yagoda.

The 409-page soft bound volume includes more than two dozen pages of photographs from the life of beloved humorist and entertainer Will Rogers, described as "an irresistible personi-fication of America." The author's comprehensive research is evident by his 49 pages of citations and references.

Rogers was born in 1879 and he died in 1935 with Wiley Post when their airplane went down in the sea near Barrow, Alaska. Before that final flight, "Will was completely taken with Alaska. And what was there not to love? By necessity, it was the most aviation-minded area in the country. And it was the final out-post of wilderness, the last place not yet conquered by so-called civilization. 'This Alaska is great country,' he told his read-ers [he was a columnist for the *New York Times*]. 'If they can just keep from being taken over by the U.S., they got a great future.'"

Trading Credit Policy

A Novel View accepts books on trade for in-store credit when the books are in good condition, in demand, and we have room on our shelves.

When we accept your books, you receive up to 25% of the origi-nal cover price for credit toward in-store purchases of used books. Credit is good toward 90% of the purchase price, with 10% in cash. Some new inventory or specially marked books, as well as featured art, are cash only purchases. We accept checks, VISA, and MasterCard for any purchase.

Frequently Asked Questions (FAQs)

Let us know your questions and we'll address them in future news-letters.

Q: *Do you have gift certificates?*

A: Yes, just ask and specify the amount.

Q: *Can you order a book for me that I haven't been able to find?*

A: Yes. We'll help locate and order the book for you.

Q: *Were you previously in the Northway Mall?*

A: Yes. In April 2001, we bought the former Gulliver's Used Books in the Northway Mall. The store's name was changed to A Novel View and remained in the Mall until April 2002. At that time, we moved to our present location in west downtown Anchorage at 415 L Street.

Q: *Where can I park downtown when I come to A Novel View?*

A: We have free parking next to the bookstore. To get to it, turn into the alley just west of the Captain Cook parking garage from either 4th or 5th Avenue, then swing through the parking lot and pull up alongside of our building. All other spaces in the parking lot are leased to other tenants.

At Your Service

It is our sincere commitment to provide customer satisfaction. Please let us know how we can be of service.

Pat Tegtmeier, Owner;
Matt Tegtmeier, Manager

Email: anovelview@msn.com
or tegthome@worldnet.att.net

Website: www.homestead.com/anovelview

Phone/Fax: (907) 278-0084

Hours

September through May:

- Monday–Friday   11:00 a.m. to 7:00 p.m.
- Saturday   10:00 a.m. to 5:00 p.m.
- Sunday   Closed

June through August:

- Monday–Friday   11:00 a.m. to 8:00 p.m.
- Saturday–Sunday   10:00 a.m. to 6:00 p.m.

What's Great About This Newsletter?

Pat obviously knows her marketplace and directs customers to the events in her store and area. As you read the newsletter consider the things that make it an excellent example:

- The first sentence creates a welcoming image of her bookstore.

- She immediately hooks her reader with a reason to come in on Valentine's Day to get a special treat.

- The paragraphs are short and easy to read.

- The information is timely and pertinent.

- She links to her website in the newsletter! Very important.

- She gives the bookstore's phone number, address, and parking directions.

- Her style is friendly, warm and makes the reader feel like a visit to A Novel View will be fun and friendly.

- She highlights books about Alaska — sure to appeal to her Anchorage readers.

- She features specific books and gets the reader excited about them.

How To Get Started with Your Own Newsletter

To get started with your own newsletter, take out your store's calendar. What is coming up that is particularly thrilling? Mention that first. What books are you really excited about? Talk about those books, maybe even with a synopsis or brief review. What on-going clubs or meetings would customers enjoy? What store benefits (like regular discounts for seniors or a book buying club) do you want to remind customers about?

List great features about your store that customers may have forgotten about or may be unaware of. Remember to link to your bookstore's website and give other pertinent contact information. Make it easy for customers to get information and to buy!

Finally, when your newsletter is complete, have several trusted individuals read it, and read it again, for spelling, grammar, and content errors. Then, get out your email mailing list and press the send button!

5.5.6 Ongoing Marketing

In Chapter 4 you learned the basics of how to advertise through print, radio, television, and the Internet. After your bookstore is open, you will still need to advertise to continue the buzz you started before you opened. But how? As you move forward with your ongoing advertising plan, consider some of these ideas:

- Mailings

- Sending birthday cards or coupons to frequent customers

- Postcards announcing special events

- Monthly store calendars

- Flyers

- Brochures

- Billboards

- In-store event bulletin board

- Trading advertising flyers with other local businesses

- Advertising in local school or college papers

- Sponsoring a sports team or advertising at a college sporting event

- A buyers club discount plan

As you try things – different forms of advertising, promotions, and events – you will begin to notice what works and what doesn't. The best way to successfully market your business is to carefully watch the results of those things you try and do whatever attracts new customers.

5.6 Customer Relations

5.6.1 Building Relationships

Building a personal relationship with customers will make your store a place that people remember and return to. In a competitive market with superstores and Internet bookstores to contend with, an ability to build personal relationships is one of the great things that an independent bookseller can do that the "big guys" simply cannot.

I had a memorable experience once at Dirk Cable's bookstore in Pasadena, California. I was taking a stroll during my lunch hour and I came across a little shop called, "Dirk Cable, Bookseller." I walked inside the beautifully appointed shop, with gleaming wooden shelves full of completely organized books, all in perfect order.

I was hoping to find something really enjoyable to read in the area I collect — children's series fiction from the 1900s on. I was greeted by Dirk Cable himself, who was accessible to customers and very interested in my questions.

After asking me a few friendly questions about the books I read and having a pleasant conversation with me, I asked him to help me find something I would enjoy. He began to look knowingly through his shelves and hand-picked books that he thought I would like. He selected two beautiful books in excellent condition for me, and I bought them both.

Dirk Cable made me feel like I was important and that he could help me find books that were exactly right for me. I felt like I found a person who understood the books I loved and was well versed in them. I left his store feeling like I had not only encountered a wonderful bookstore, but had also made a new literary friend.

You don't need an intuitive sense about how to build relationships with customers. By following just a few simple rules, you can create relationships with almost everyone who comes through your door. Consider the following methods to build great customer relationships:

Be Accessible

It isn't enough to be present; you have to be accessible. Do you know someone in a work or personal situation who is around but is always too busy to deal with you?

As a bookseller, you will have to do a number of pressing things that will take you away from the bookstore floor, but when you are on the floor, make sure you are available. Your customers want to know you are available to answer their questions. If you are with another customer, greet the person waiting, make eye contact, and tell them you will be happy to help them in just a moment. And then keep your promise.

Take an Interest

There is no substitute for caring. If you actually take an interest in the customers who come into your store, they will instantly know it. There is no magic to retail relationship building — it works the same way you build any other relationship. You have to be aware of who comes into your store. Treat questions as if they are very important to you. Make it clear to your customers that you care about what they need.

One important skill that all customer service experts share is the ability to listen carefully to the customers they are trying to help. You can't help customers unless you know what they need. Sometimes learning to listen will take some time, but as you try it, and really try to let people tell you what they need, you will find your skills improve.

Learn Names

Even if you are terrible at names, figure out a way to learn the names of your customers. Introduce yourself and ask for customers' names, too. Then commit the names to memory. You might have to ask a couple times, or you might have to use a little mental word association.

Get to Know People

If you get to know your bookstore customers, you will find out about who they are as readers, what books they love, and what books they are looking for. When you know that, you can make personal suggestions.

It is flattering for customers when a bookseller has something in mind for them based on prior discussions. Personal suggestions are sure-fire ways of letting your customers know they matter.

It is also wonderful to make a personal connection. Ask Bob Smith how his son did in the football game. Ask Teresa Banks how her ailing mother is doing. Wish someone a happy birthday. Remember that you have a chance to build community around you. Customers are the lifeblood of a bookstore — treat them like they are worth knowing.

Be Knowledgeable

Customers will ask your advice about books to buy. Keeping informed of industry news can help you give them the advice they are seeking. Another thing that most booksellers do is get their staff involved. You can definitely get the people who work for you to read books and reviews. This is an excellent way to delegate a giant task and make sure your staff stays knowledgeable.

Personal attention is one of the most important things that an independent bookstore can offer that a chain or superstore can't. Your staff can become the experts that customers will rely on for information about what they should read.

Do the One Extra Thing

Every time you deal with a customer, do that one extra thing. Whether it means looking up a book for a customer, making a call regarding a book you don't have, or even finding a special bow for a wrapped gift — find one special thing you can do for each customer and do it. It is a great way to ensure a customer leaves your store happy. If you can make sure that everyone leaves your store with the words "Wasn't that nice?" in their mind and on their lips, you will have a successful store.

5.6.2 Working with Customers for Feedback

Remember the old saying, "The customer is always right"? Whether or not you subscribe to this saying, one thing is true: Customers can and will give you feedback — about your bookstore, what they like, what they don't like, and what they want. They are an excellent source of feedback that will help you assess your bookstore's success.

Probably the best way to tell if customers like what you are doing is whether or not they are buying. But even if customers aren't buying, it doesn't mean they don't want to. Your goal should be to find out what they do want to buy, what motivates them, and what keeps them from buying.

There are a variety of ways to get feedback from your customers — some more formal than others. First and foremost, you can always just talk to them. If you adopt a friendly attitude toward your customers every day, you can always get feedback whenever you need it. Listen to what they have to say, and remember that even negative feedback is just information. It is infinitely helpful to have people willing to tell you what they think — no matter what it is.

Customer Feedback Form

If you prefer a more anonymous way of dealing with customers, or feel you might get more real feedback if they can give you their opinions anonymously, then consider a customer feedback form. This can be as simple as something you write up on your computer or as formal as something you might bring to your printer.

You can place these at your cash register with a small sign — just ask your staff to ask customers to fill out a form. Have a sealed container or another special place that you place the forms until you are ready to review them. A sample feedback form is included on the next two pages.

TIP: Give customers a little gift for filling out your feedback form — perhaps a free cookie from your café, or a store bookmark as a way of saying thank you.

Customer Focus Group

Ask customers who feel at home in your store if they would be willing to come together in discussion groups. One excellent way to get a focus group together is to ask the members of one of your book club groups. After all, they are already coming to your store at a specified time to discuss books, which makes them the perfect group with whom to begin a discussion.

Sample Customer Feedback Form

We at Grace's Book Gallery are always interested in what our customers are thinking and feeling about our bookstore. Please take a minute and let us know what we can do to make your book buying experience more positive.

Thank you for your help,
The Management of Grace's Book Gallery

Please circle from 1 (poor) to 5 (excellent) for each question.

Our Staff

What kind of job does our staff do at the following things?

1. Greeting you when you come into our bookstore   1 2 3 4 5

2. Being available to answer your questions   1 2 3 4 5

3. Leaving you alone so you can browse in peace   1 2 3 4 5

4. Making you aware of books or new releases you might like   1 2 3 4 5

5. Helping you with questions   1 2 3 4 5

6. Helping you with problems or concerns   1 2 3 4 5

7. Making you feel at home in our store   1 2 3 4 5

Our Selection

What kind of a job are we doing with the following things?

1. Having new books available for you in a timely manner   1 2 3 4 5

2. Making you aware of up and coming books   1 2 3 4 5

3. Helping you order books we don't have   1 2 3 4 5

4. Getting special orders to you quickly   1 2 3 4 5

Your Comfort and Enjoyment

How are we doing with the following things?

1. Enough places for you to sit and read   1 2 3 4 5

2. A comfortable place to get a cup of coffee   1 2 3 4 5
   and a snack

3. Menu items you enjoy at reasonable prices   1 2 3 4 5

4. Making you feel welcome   1 2 3 4 5

5. Interesting events and classes   1 2 3 4 5

Other Areas

1. Is there anything you would like to see change?
   _____
   _____

2. Is there anything missing?
   _____
   _____

3. Other thoughts?
   _____
   _____

4. Would you like to be contacted regarding anything?   *Yes No*

5. Would you like to be added to our mailing list or   *Yes No*
   email newsletter?

Name: _____

Address: _____

Phone: _____

Email: _____

Thank you for your help!

Even if you don't want to set up a full-fledged focus group, you might just drop in on a book club group and ask them if they have time to answer a question or two. Or have coffee and cake after the group meets and use this as a less formal way to ask their opinions.

Your Website and Customer Feedback

Another excellent way to connect with customers and get their feedback is through your bookstore's website. Some customers enjoy answering questions in the comfort and solitude of their own homes, and a simple way to do this is to put a form on your site that allows them to submit their feedback online.

6. Staying Competitive

There is more to your bookstore than coming to work every day and selling books. You must stay competitive if you are going to succeed in today's book industry market.

This means that you must carefully plan your strategy to succeed, and you must be willing to change your plans if they aren't working. Only through careful and honest review of how you are doing can you continue to change with the times and ensure your bookstore's continued success.

6.1 Evaluating and Assessing Operations

People always say, "Don't look for problems." In the case of your bookstore's operations, you must review and evaluate all aspects of your bookstore to find and solve the problems.

As you look at your financial reports that you generate weekly and monthly, you will begin to see trends — ultimately you will see if you are making money or losing money. Any assessment consideration about your bookstore must be linked to this. Your number one concern is making a profit.

What Are You Doing Right and Wrong?

Sales

- What are your weekly sales figures? Monthly?

- Are they up or down from the week before or the month before?

- What is causing this?

- Are there seasonal or holiday considerations?

Advertising, Marketing, and Promotions

- Is your advertising working?

- Are you measuring your ad response?

- Have you published a coupon that customers can bring into your store?

- Is your staff aware of promotions and actively presenting them to customers?

Staff

- Are your staff members making or breaking sales?

- Are they friendly and informed?

- Are they being courteous to customers and helping them with questions?

A poor sales staff can definitely hurt your overall sales. Also, consider getting yourself a personal mystery shopper — a trusted, personal friend who will come into your store, pretend to be a customer, and give you feedback about their experience.

Events

- Are you scheduling events?

- Are they well attended?

- Do you have a guest book for each event or are you counting the number of people that attend?

- Are you making more sales on event days?

- Are you getting press coverage for your events?

Physical Store

- How does your store look?

- Is it inviting?

- Is it neat and well-cared-for?

- Is it organized?

- Are you using effective window displays and feature displays?

- Are they helping you to sell books?

Operational Techniques

- Are you keeping good records?

- Are you seeing mistakes in your daily cash reports?

- Are you remembering to run and review your daily, weekly, and monthly reports?

- Is your staff trained well enough so they don't make any large or costly errors?

What Else?

Give yourself time each week — or each day — to think about what happened in your store and where you noticed problems. As you review the areas above, make a list of what you need to change and how you will change it. Hold regular team meetings to make your staff aware of changes they need to make in the way your bookstore does business.

6.2 Increasing or Decreasing by Category

One of the great things about having an organized inventory and using effective inventory software will be your ability to see your bookstore's sales results by category. This is a vital aspect of any bookstore's inventory management. You need to be able to evaluate clearly which book categories are selling and which are not.

Check your daily, weekly, and monthly sales. After a few months, you should be able to see trends. And after one year in operation, you will be able to see changes that happen to your bookstore's sales during seasonal and holiday times.

Begin to think about increasing or decreasing categories by the sales performance of individual categories. Some booksellers say this is where they have some surprises. Sometimes your best-laid plans are just wrong — and there is nothing like a sales report to give you that information. If a category isn't producing any sales, you should think about how to better spend your inventory dollars in that area.

Consider the following tips for evaluating your categories before you decide to increase or decrease them:

- Which category in your store has the most sales on a consistent basis?

- Is this the category you predicted would be the best sales producer?

- Which category in your store has the least sales on a consistent basis?

- Is this the category that you predicted would sell the least?
- How attached are you to the floundering category?

- Do you feel the category gives your store meaning in some way?

- Have you been promoting the books in that category through advertising or feature displays or on your website?

- Do you see a way to increase your most successful category?

- Are there more books in this category that you have been hesitating to buy?

Creating the right mix of categories is sort of like being a master chef. You have to play with your category recipe until you find the perfect blend that satisfies your customers and meets your expectations for your bookstore's vision.

Remember that, like all aspects of your bookstore, you will have to "tweak" it and change it until it works. You may have to change it again based on current events or how the demographics of your bookstore's neighborhood changes over time. Being constantly aware of how your categories perform will help you to make the best choices.

TIP: Remember that you can return and exchange books with many publishers. This allows you to quickly add to a category and subtract from another, or even remove a category and add a new one. Make sure you are clear about return policy details before you buy from every new publisher.

6.3 Implementing Change

One thing that successful bookstore owners seem to agree upon is that their businesses don't stay the same — they grow and change and evolve.

Many of the booksellers interviewed for this book told stories of those changes and how they improved their stores by paying attention to the things changing around them — from their customers to their community to world events. They have become increasingly aware of how they can change things about their stores and move along with the rest of the world.

Bookstores, more than most retail businesses, have the chance to stay current and keep up with new ideas by the very nature of the product — books. Bookstore owners sell ideas. It's an amazing business to be in.

As you go through the adventure of owning your own bookstore, be open to the learning experience. Become an open-minded bookseller. Be open to changes, open to improvements, open to technology, and open to ideas. This is the true way to harness success.

And finally, enjoy the process and know that you are doing what most people only dream about. You are living your dream — opening your own bookstore!

Remember these tips:

C • Change with the times; be open to your customers, create something new and exciting in your bookstore.

H • Hear what customers are saying; be happy to help people find the ideas, solutions and new worlds that they seek in books.

A • Alert yourself to new trends, amaze your customers by helping them to stay aware of what is new and exciting in the world, and use your bookstore as a catalyst for community movement and growth.

N • Never stop learning, immerse yourself in what is new in the world that will improve your store, access learning opportunities through the national and regional booksellers associations, say "yes" to learning as a business owner and a bookseller.

G • Give of yourself. Give your insight and wisdom to your staff, your knowledge, friendship and opinions to your customers. Give back to the community that your bookstore calls home. Remember that giving back will always bring you more success.

E • Explore. Be willing to do the new and exciting, to take risks, to do the unexpected, to explore new bookstore events, capture and present trends even before they're hot, and to see what is coming before your competition. Give your creative spirit free reign as a bookseller.

7. Resources

As you have noticed, throughout the book, there are a variety of interesting links to websites that can be of assistance to you in your quest to open your own bookstore. Below you will find a number of other important links that will help the new bookseller.

7.1 Professional Associations

National Associations

- *American Booksellers Association (ABA)*
  www.bookweb.org

- *Antiquarian Booksellers Association of Canada (A.B.A.C.)*
  www.abac.org/english.html

- *Book and Periodical Council — Canada*
  www.bookandperiodicalcouncil.ca

- *Book Industry Study Group*
  www.bisg.org

- *Canadian Booksellers Association (C.B.A.)*
  www.cbabook.org/main/default.asp

- *Independent Online Booksellers Association*
  www.ioba.org/index.html

- *International League of Antiquarian Booksellers (I.L.A.B.)*
  www.ilab-lila.com

Regional Associations

- *Pacific Northwest Booksellers Association (PNBA)*
  www.pnba.org

- *Northern California Independent Booksellers Association (NCIBA)*
  www.nciba.com

- *Southern California Booksellers Association (SCBA)*
  www.scbabooks.org

- *Mountain Plains Booksellers Association (MPBA)*
  www.mountainsplains.org

- *Mid-South Independent Booksellers Association (MSIBA)*
  www.msiba.org

- *Upper Midwest Booksellers Association (UMBA)*
  www.abookaday.com

- *Great Lakes Booksellers Association (GLBA)*
  www.books-glba.org/index00.php

- *New England Booksellers Association (NEBA)*
  www.newenglandbooks.org

- *New Atlantic Independent Booksellers Association (NAIBA)*
  www.newatlanticbooks.com

- *Southeast Booksellers Association (SEBA)*
  www.sebaweb.org

7.2 Online Resources

Directories

- *BookWire™ Mailing List Index*
  www.bookwire.com/bookwire/lit.listserv.html

- *Links to Canadian Used Rare and Antiquarian Booksellers*
  www.ramsaybooks.com/bookstore/dealinks.html

Reviews and Publications

- *Bookpage — America's Book Review*
  www.bookpage.com

- *BookSpot.com — Book Related Content Online*
  www.bookspot.com

- *BookWire — The Book Industry Resource*
  www.bookwire.com

- *Library Journal*
  www.libraryjournal.com

- *New York Review of Books*
  www.nybooks.com

- *Publisher's Weekly*
  www.publishersweekly.com

- *School Library Journal*
  www.schoollibraryjournal.com

- *The Sunday Times Book Review*
  www.nytimes.com/pages/books/review/index.html

- *Publisher's Lunch*
  (Free daily newsletter delivered by email.)
  www.caderbooks.com

Best-Seller Lists

- *Random House: The Modern Library 100 Best Novels of All Time*
  www.randomhouse.com/modernlibrary/100bestnovels.html

- *USA Today's Top 150 Best-Selling Books List*
  www.usatoday.com/life/books/top-50.htm

- *The New York Times Best-Seller Lists*
  www.nytimes.com/pages/books/bestseller

More Fabulous Books

Find out how to break into the "fab" job of your dreams with FabJob.com career guides. Each 2-in-1 set includes a print book and CD-ROM.

Start Your Own Coffee House

By owning your own coffee house, you become part of a rich culture. In our culture, coffee is seen as social, affluent, and hip. **FabJob Guide to Become a Coffee House Owner** shows you how to:

- Your options for buying an existing coffee house, franchising, or opening a new coffee house
- How to build a coffee house (including how to find the right location and avoid costly mistakes)
- How to save money on equipment for your café
- How to market your coffee house to attract customers
- Financing your coffee house business and managing your money

Get Paid to Plan Events

Imagine having an exciting high paying job that lets you use your creativity to organize fun and important events. **FabJob Guide to Become an Event Planner** shows you how to:

- Teach yourself event planning (includes step-by-step advice for planning an event)
- Make your event a success and avoid disasters
- Get a job as an event planner with a corporation, convention center, country club, tourist attraction, resort or other event industry employer
- Start your own event planning business, price your services, and find clients
- Be certified as a professional event planner

Visit www.FabJob.com to order guides today!

Does Someone You Love Deserve a Fab Job?

Giving a FabJob® guide is a fabulous way to show someone you believe in them and support their dreams. Help them break into the career of their dreams with the ...

- FabJob Guide to **Become a Bed and Breakfast Owner**
- FabJob Guide to **Become a Business Consultant**
- FabJob Guide to **Become a Caterer**
- FabJob Guide to **Become a Celebrity Personal Assistant**
- FabJob Guide to **Become a Children's Book Author**
- FabJob Guide to **Become an Event Planner**
- FabJob Guide to **Become an Etiquette Consultant**
- FabJob Guide to **Become a Fashion Designer**
- FabJob Guide to **Become a Florist**
- FabJob Guide to **Become a Human Resources Specialist**
- FabJob Guide to **Become a Makeup Artist**
- FabJob Guide to **Become a Massage Therapist**
- FabJob Guide to **Become a Model**
- FabJob Guide to **Become a Motivational Speaker**
- FabJob Guide to **Become a Personal Shopper**
- FabJob Guide to **Become a Professional Organizer**
- FabJob Guide to **Become a Public Relations Consultant**
- FabJob Guide to **Become a Super Salesperson**
- **And dozens more fabulous careers!**

Visit FabJob.com for details and special offers

Tell Us What You Think

Would you like to share your thoughts with other FabJob readers? Please contact us at **www.FabJob.com/feedback.asp** to tell us how this guide has helped prepare you for your dream career. If we publish your comments on our website or in our promotional materials, we will send you a gift certificate for 50% off your next purchase of a FabJob guide.

Remember that if you want us to be able to publish your feedback, include your full name and city of residence, and limit your comments to 200 words. We appreciate you taking the time to contact us, and look forward to hearing from you.

The FabJob Newsletter

Get valuable career advice for **free** by subscribing to the FabJob newsletter. You'll receive insightful tips on:

- how to break into the job of your dreams or start the business of your dreams

- how to avoid career mistakes

- how to increase your on-the-job satisfaction and success

You'll also receive discounts on FabJob guides, and be the first to know about upcoming titles. Subscribe to the FabJob newsletter at **www. FabJob.com/signup_site.asp**